Habits *of a* Loving Heart

Habits of a Loving Heart

WILLARD TATE

Christian Communications
P.O. Box 150
Nashville, Tennessee 37202

Copyright © 1992 by Gospel Advocate Co.

IT IS ILLEGAL AND UNETHICAL TO DUPLICATE COPYRIGHTED MATERIAL.

The material in this study represents a considerable investment of effort, skill, time, and finances from both the author and the publisher. If this material is photocopied and circulated to avoid buying a book for each student, the author is defrauded of duly earned royalties, and the publisher does not sell enough copies to support the publication.

All rights reserved. No part of this publication may be reproduced, stored in a retrieval system, or transmitted in any form or by any means—electronic, mechanical, photocopy, recording, or any other—except for brief quotations in printed reviews, without the prior permission of the publisher.

All Scripture quotations are from the Holy Bible New International Version, Copyright 1978, New York Bible Society. Used by permission.

Published by Christian Communications
A division of the Gospel Advocate Co.
P. O. Box 150, Nashville, TN 37202

ISBN 0-89225-411-4

DEDICATION

I dedicate this book to my wife, Bobbie, and Larry Weeden of *Focus on the Family*. You are my heroes.

Bobbie, I also dedicated my first book, *Learning to Love*, to you because of your unique ability to love as a wife and mother. Now I acknowledge your pricelss help to me in writing these books.

Larry very capably edits my books with an extraordinary combination of the skills of a professional editor and the understanding of the subject.

You both remind me of the song *Wind Beneath My Wings* by Gary Morris. To most you are only a name, but I never once heard you complain. You always walked a step behind, content to let me shine. because of your strength and skill, I am the one with all the glory. But I would be nothing without you.

You are everything I'd like to be. Thanks for helping me fly.

CONTENTS

1. Habits of a Loving Heart 1
2. Doing the Right Thing for the Right Reason 7
3. Giving the Gift of Courtesy 21
4. Rejoicing, Not Resentful 34
5. Showing True Humility 46
6. Encouraging Others 58
7. Keeping a Long Fuse 70
8. Holds No Grudges 81
9. Drawn to the Truth 90
10. Always Optimistic 103
11. Willingness to Persevere 115
12. Never Lets Others Down 124
13. You Can't Live Any Better Than You Can Love 135

1

Habits of a Loving Heart

Love is the only spiritual power that can overcome the self-centeredness inherent in being alive. Love is the thing that makes life possible, or, indeed, tolerable.
(Arnold Toynbee)

John Powell told the story of Norma Jean Mortenson. She was one of the most famous people of this century but also one of the most tragic. Her mother, Gladys Baker, was committed to mental institutions many times, and Norma Jean spent much of her childhood in foster homes.

In one of those homes, when she was 8 years old, a boarder in the house raped her, then gave her a nickel and said, "Here, Honey, take this, and don't ever tell anybody what I did to you."

She did report the crime to her foster mother, however, but the response was not what you would expect. The woman beat Norma Jean badly and told her, "Our boarder pays good rent, and don't you ever say anything bad about him!" So at the tender age of 8, the girl learned what it is to be used and bought off and beaten for trying to express your hurt.

As time passed, Norma Jean became a pretty young woman, and people began to notice. When boys whistled, she enjoyed it, but she wished they would notice her as a person, too, not just an attractive face and body.

Then Norma Jean went to Hollywood to become an actress.

The publicity people told her, "We're going to make a modern sex symbol out of you."

"A cymbal?" she said. "Cymbals are things people hit together, aren't they?"

"Honey," they answered, "it doesn't matter, because we're going to make you the most sizzling sex symbol to ever hit Hollywood."

After she changed her name to Marilyn Monroe, that prophecy pretty much came true. She was an overnight movie sensation in dumb blonde roles. But always she kept asking, "Can't you see that I'm a person, not just a face and body? Would you please notice?"

> *Feeling loved is the greatest feeling in the world.*

Marilyn soon became known as a selfish prima donna. She gave film crews all kinds of trouble on movie sets, often making them wait hours before she was ready to perform. What they didn't know was that she was in her dressing room vomiting because she was terrified.

No one took her seriously. She went through three marriages in search of a man who would love her as a person. Her desperate pleas for respect and a chance to become a genuine actress went unheeded.

Finally, on a Sunday night at the age of 35, when beautiful women are supposed to be in the arms of people who love them, Marilyn Monroe took her own life. When the maid found her body the next morning, she noticed the phone was off the hook, dangling beside the tragic star. Later investigation revealed that in the last moments of her life, Marilyn had called a Hollywood actor and told him she had taken enough sleeping pills to kill herself.

His response typified so much of the pain in her life. Using the famous line of Rhett Butler in the movie *Gone with the Wind* (edited here), he had told her, "Frankly, my dear, I don't care." Those were the last words she heard.

Later, in an article, Clare Booth Luce asked, "What really killed Marilyn Monroe, the love goddess who never found any love?" She reasoned rightly that the dangling phone was a symbol of Marilyn's life; she died because she never got through to anyone who understood. She never, in her entire life, felt really loved.

Don't you wish someone had taken little Norma Jean Mortenson to Sunday school and church and just loved her and taught her to sing "Jesus loves me, this I know"? But instead, Marilyn Monroe's life stands as a painfully clear illustration of a central truth of human existence: You can't live any better than you can love and be loved. All the fame and fortune in the world can never satisfy the person without love. The human spirit needs love just as much as the body needs food and water.

> *Jesus calls on all His disciples to love one another.*

Furthermore, Jesus calls on all His disciples to love one another; in fact, He said that's how people will know we're His followers (see John 13:34,35). He even tells us to love our enemies and those who mistreat us (see Luke 6:27-35).

That's why I never get tired of talking about love—the subject will never fade in importance, and it's impossible to exhaust the topic. Can you think of a more important subject we could explore together? I can't.

Bill Bright, founder and president of Campus Crusade for Christ, is often asked to speak to various groups. He speaks about reaching the world for Christ and living in obedience to God's Word under the direction of the Holy Spirit. He addresses those same topics over and over.

One time he was asked why he speaks repeatedly on those

themes when there are so many others he could discuss. "Sure, I could talk about a lot of things," he said, "but there are none more important than fulfilling the Great Commission and living a Spirit-filled life. Those are the things God has called me to preach and teach."

God has also given me a sense of mission—a mission which includes the above but also is a mission to help us all learn how to love the way He wants.

I write and talk about what I want to learn, and I really want to learn to love. Do you? This book is titled *Habits of a Loving Heart* because it describes 12 traits of a truly loving heart—of a heart filled with the love and joy God wants for all of us. If you find all 12 are always true of the way you love, congratulations—you're ready for heaven! But if you're like the rest of us, you'll see at least one, maybe several, areas where there's room for improvement.

My goal is not to make anyone feel guilty or unworthy because of their failing in some area. Instead, it is to encourage each one to pick out one of the habits we need to develop and start working on it. God will help us in our sincere efforts to please Him. We know, after all, that "he who began a good work in you will carry it on to completion until the day of Christ Jesus" (Philippians 1:6).

These 12 habits of a loving heart actually come from the One who knows more about love than anyone else, and more specifically from that part of His Word known as the love chapter (1 Corinthians 13). It's a familiar passage, but I believe we can see some truths in it that may have escaped notice before. Learning and developing these habits will make a truly loving heart.

The story is told that on one of his many plane trips, the late, great General Omar Bradley, one of the American heroes of World War II, was in a business suit rather than his Army uniform. As he took his seat and got out some papers to work on, he saw that seated next to him was a young Army private. The soldier proved to be a friendly Gomer Pyle-type who wanted to strike up a conversation.

"Since we're going to be traveling together," the private

said, "it would be nice for us to get to know each other. I take it you're a banker in the city."

Bradley was tired but still wanted to get some work done, and the last thing he wanted was a cocky, young soldier talking to him throughout the flight. Hoping to intimidate the private into silence, he answered, "No, young man, I'm not a banker. I happen to be General Omar Bradley, a five-star general in the U.S. Army. I'm also chairman of the Joint Chiefs of Staff at the Pentagon in Washington, D.C."

His words failed to achieve his purpose. The young man responded, "Wow! That sounds like a very important job, sir. I just hope you don't blow it!"

I also have a very important job in writing about love. So much has already been said about it, but it's such a crucial and deep subject that I think we should all continue seeking to explore it.

A cartoon by Michael Maslin showed a middle-class man in a middle-class living room watching a middle-class T.V. set. On the screen was a large cooking pot, and the off-camera voice was saying, "How much would you pay for all the secrets of the universe? But wait! Don't answer yet! If you buy now, you'll also get this six-quart combination spaghetti pot and clam steamer. Now how much would you pay?"

For a lot less than the cost of a six-quart spaghetti pot and clam steamer, you've bought this book that distills what God has taught me about the nature of love. So let's continue to explore together the habits of a loving heart.

Chapter Reflection

The story of Norma Jean Mortenson is a sad story indeed. What was the point of the story? Could her life have taken a different direction? How?

Discussion Questions

1. Can you share other stories similar to Norma Jean's?
2. Do you agree with the author's statement "You can't live any better than you can love and be loved?" Does love make that kind of difference? Explain.
3. Read Luke 6:27-31. What is involved in loving those who do not love you? Think of personal examples.

2

Doing the Right Thing for the Right Reason

*The Light of Lights
Looks always on the motive,
not the deed,
The Shadow of Shadows on the deed alone.*
                              (William Butler Yeats)

Students enroll in college for many reasons. Even the good students, the ones who work hard to make the most of their opportunities, put in the long hours for a variety of reasons. One student, whom I'll never forget, was there for the best reason possible.

Soap Pich was from Cambodia. As did the rest of the class, early in the term he gave his lifeline, or brief life's story, in front of the class. Soap said that when he was about 5 years old, his family enjoyed a middle-class lifestyle, which meant a lot of luxury and social prestige in Cambodia. But when the communists took control of the country, they immediately rounded up all of the rich and/or educated men and led them to a field where they were shot like animals.

Fortunately, Soap's father was one of the few people spared. He was needed by the communists because of his ability to keep the phone system working. However, he was closely guarded while he was working; and the family was also under constant observation. Soap told the class about how his father would play with him and the family dog his dad loved so much. When his father would go to the store on his scooter, the dog would ride with him. When his dad bought sunglasses or a hat for himself, he'd buy the same for his dog.

Then one day, Soap said, when they were returning from the store, the communists captured him and took him away. He never saw him again.

"You mean the dog?" the class asked.

"No, my dad," Soap answered.

Soap was about 7 at that time. The communists separated the rest of the family after that, so Soap was alone. He told the class how he cried himself to sleep every night for three months afterward.

Soap said that there had been only one guard watching his father when he was out working on the phone lines. At any time, his father could have overtaken the guard and made his escape, but the guard had repeatedly told him, "If you run, we'll kill your family." His father had seen it happen many times, and he didn't doubt they would carry out their threat. So he chose to stay to protect his family and, by doing so, lost his life.

Miraculously, Soap and the rest of his family escaped to America, and that's how he came to be a student in my class. "My dad died so I could live," he told the students in conclusion, "and he always wanted me to get an education."

What kind of student do you suppose Soap was? How hard do you think he worked to take full advantage of what his father died to make possible? *Love* motivated his dad to give himself, and *love* motivated Soap to give his best effort day after day.

It's entirely possible, of course, to do even the right thing for the wrong reason. A perfect example of that is found in John 8:1-11. Some "teachers of the law" and Pharisees brought to Jesus a woman who had been caught in adultery. It was right and proper that she (and the man involved) be punished for her immorality.

But why did those men bring her to Jesus? He wasn't a judge. Were they concerned mostly with seeing the Law of Moses upheld? Did they want the woman to experience the forgiveness of sins Jesus was preaching about? No, their reason was that they were hoping Jesus would say or do something that would allow them to accuse *Him* of violating the law. Their only goal was to create an incident over which they could condemn Him. The fate of the woman, physically or spiritually, was of no real concern to them. Love played *no part* in their motivation.

> *The loving heart seeks to do things for the right reasons.*

The loving heart consistently seeks to do things for the right reason. As the Lord told the prophet Samuel, "The Lord does not look at the things man looks at. Man looks at the outward appearance, but the Lord looks at the heart" (1 Samuel 16:7). Our motivation for what we do means everything to Him.

Jesus' Clear Teaching

Jesus made the importance of our reasons for what we do and say unmistakably clear. "Be careful not to do your 'acts of righteousness' before men, to be seen by them," He said in Matthew 6:1. "If you do, you will have no reward from your Father in heaven." In other words, doing the right things in order to receive the praise of other people will get you that and nothing else.

Then He talked about three different kinds of good things we can do, things very important to devout Jews. First, He said, "When you give to the needy, do not announce it with trumpets, as the hypocrites do in the synagogues and on the streets, to be honored by men. I tell you the truth, they have received their reward in full. But when you give to the needy, do not let your left hand know what your right hand is doing, so that your giving may be in secret. Then your Father, who sees what is done in secret, will reward you" (Matthew 6:2-4).

Next, He said this about prayer: "When you pray, do not be like the hypocrites, for they love to pray standing in the synagogues and on the street corners to be seen by men. I tell you the truth, they have received their reward in full. When you pray, go into your room, close the door and pray to your Father, who is unseen. Then your Father, who sees what is done in secret, will reward you" (Matthew 6:5,6).

Finally, Jesus said about fasting: "When you fast, do not look somber as the hypocrites do, for they disfigure their faces to show men they are fasting. I tell you the truth, they have received their reward in full. But when you fast, put oil on your head and wash your face [in other words, dress and groom yourself just like always], so that it will not be obvious to men that you are fasting, but only to your Father, who is unseen; and your Father, who sees what is done in secret, will reward you" (Matthew 6:16-18).

Giving to the needy, praying and fasting are three important practices, not only to ancient (and modern) Jews, but also to Christians. Yet, even such pious activities (not to mention teaching Sunday school, leading singing, preaching, etc.) can be done for the wrong reasons. And Jesus made it perfectly clear what we can expect if we try to serve and worship Him for any reason other than love. In the first three verses of 1 Corinthians 13, Paul listed a number of outstandingly good things a person can do or possess: (1) speak in the tongues of angels, (2) have all knowledge and great faith and (3) give your life for the cause of Christ. Yet, he concluded, "If I . . . have not love, I gain nothing."

Unfortunately, there's a gospel of success that preaches well to an eager audience in America today. Serve God, says this heresy, and He'll make and keep you healthy, happy and financially prosperous. But try selling that to Jesus' loyal followers in Africa, in China, in South America or in much of our own country where poverty is a common way of life. No, the rewards of God are not primarily material. If we look back at Matthew 5 and the beatitudes, we see Jesus offering such spiritual rewards as comfort, righteousness, mercy and the privilege of being called God's children.

When Love Is the Motivation

What happens when love is our main motivation? What practical effects does it have in our lives? Let's look at several things that occur.

First, the goal of loving others will give our lives meaning. I spend most of my time with young people, and it amazes and saddens me to see how little meaning they have. When I ask students to write their life's philosophy in my class, many of them say that's the first time they've spent even a minute thinking about it. But the happiest people in the world are those who are convinced their lives have meaning and have tailored their lives accordingly.

> *Loving others will give our lives meaning.*

Every once in a while, I'll come across a newspaper or magazine article profiling some extremely successful person in one line of work or another. This person invariably works longer and harder than 99 percent of the rest of us, week in and week out. But is the person unhappy about that? Is he or she complaining? No, the individual wouldn't have it any other way! Why? Because the person loves what he or she is doing and draws great fulfillment from it. Let me give you one such example of real success.

In an interview a few years ago, Mother Teresa of Calcutta, India—the nun who takes the dying and other unwanted people off the streets and cares for them—was asked when a typical day for her began. She answered that she started with prayer at 4:30. And what did she do after early-morning prayer?

"We try to pray through our work by doing it with Jesus, for Jesus, to Jesus. That helps us put our whole heart and soul into doing it. The dying, the crippled, the mentally ill, the unwanted, the unloved—they are Jesus in disguise" (a reference to Matthew 25:31-46: "Whatever you did for one of the least of these brothers of mine . . .").

Then she went on to explain her perspective of her life's mission: "I don't claim anything of the work. It is His [God's] work. I am like a little pencil in His hand. That is all. He does the thinking. He does the writing. The pencil has nothing to do with it. The pencil has only to be allowed to be used" (*Time*, 12/4/89, p. 11).

Does that sound like a person who is motivated by love for God and others? Of course it does. Mother Teresa has learned that working for a cause that's greater than yourself is one of the true sources of a successful, fulfilling life. And as a result, people come from all over the world to volunteer their time helping in her work. She's a poor woman who labors incredibly long and difficult hours; yet, people desperately want what she's got.

The reason is simple. Most people feel no real meaning in life; yet, deep within each of us, God has planted the truth that life *ought* to have meaning beyond "eat, drink and be merry." And until we align ourselves with that purpose, we can achieve and buy all we want, and we'll still be bored and frustrated and empty. Folks who spend their days buying cars and clothes and rings don't seem to know—or are trying hard not to admit—that empty lives are just as empty when they're filled only with material things. It's very possible to be in *Who's Who* and not know what's what.

The actor Jack Lemmon summed this all up when he said, "Like a lot of people, I used to think success meant having money or fame. And I figured it ended all your problems. It doesn't. They just change. You get some new problems just as big. A man who sweeps streets can be a success if he loves what He is doing and he does it as well as he possibly can."

Loving what you're doing and having the right motive for doing it—that's what will make you a success.

A second, related thing that love motivation will do is to give our lives direction. If we have direction, it becomes much easier to decide how best to spend our time each day. I hope you've started thinking about what kind of purpose God has for you. But how do you decide where to go from there?

It's helpful to imagine you've just been told by your doctor that you have only six months to live. I don't mean to be morbid, but given that reality, how would you choose to spend your time? What things do you know you'd just *have* to do? What things would you *like* to do? And what are some things you're already doing—maybe things that seem pretty important now—that you know you wouldn't do at all? If you answer those three questions, you'll have a good handle on what's really important and how you ought to spend your time each day.

> *It's possible to be in the Who's Who and not know What's What.*

It's amazing what we can do when we understand our priorities and are properly motivated. A humorous story is told of an important football game played by a famous college team. There were two minutes left in the game, and the team was six points ahead when they got possession of the ball again. The coach told his quarterback to play it safe and try to run out the clock, sealing the victory.

The young quarterback had ideas of his own, however. He went back to the huddle and said to his teammates, "Hey, coach says to play it safe. That's what the other team thinks we're going to do, so let's surprise them and run a pass play instead."

He threw a pass. But a defensive back from the other team (who had the speed of a sprinter) cut in front of the intended receiver, intercepted the pass, and took off running the other way for what looked like a sure, game-winning touchdown.

The quarterback, not known for being very fast, took off after the guy, ran him down and tackled him at the five-yard line. It proved to be a game-saving tackle, as their defense shut the other team down while the clock ran out.

After the game, the losing coach came up to the winner and said, "Hey, all I had heard was how slow your quarterback was; yet, he ran down my speedster!"

"Yeah," the winning coach answered, "but you have to understand. Your man was running for six points. My man was running for his *life.*"

Knowing what you're running for does make a difference. And we as Christians need to understand that we're here to make the world a better place. We do that by sharing the Gospel in love, and we do it by acting in love toward everyone we meet. Beyond that, God has a unique purpose for each of us, and we need to find it and direct our lives accordingly.

If we don't, we'll be like the hound dog that starts tracking aimlessly. First he scents a deer, and he runs that for awhile. Then he catches the trail of a jack rabbit, and next he flushes a covey of quail. By the time his owner finds him, he's barking down a gopher hole. It's so easy to follow every interesting trail that comes along and end up barking down a gopher hole when we don't have our calling and direction clearly in mind.

The third thing a goal of love will do for us is to lift us above criticism. Criticism is a part of life, especially if you try to change anything, even for the better. And handling it is so much easier if you know what you're doing and why.

You remember the story of Nehemiah, the Old Testament hero who was cupbearer to King Artaxerxes of Persia when God called him to go to Jerusalem and rebuild its walls. While he was doing that, four times his enemies came and criticized him and challenged him to come down. But all four times, he responded, "I'm doing a great work here. I can't come down."

It's so important that we, like Nehemiah, stay focused on

our God-given purpose. Yet, it's so easy to get distracted. And all too often, the things for which we're criticized and for which we criticize others in church are petty concerns. A week later, we don't even remember them, but the wounds we cause each other take years to heal.

So often the world criticizes us (and we *may* criticize others likewise) just because our meaning or direction is not understood. A great example of this is the story of the symphony orchestra that had practiced and practiced for a great concert. And in one piece, a flute player was positioned offstage so that at just the right moment, he could start playing, and his music would float in beautifully from the side. Since he couldn't see the conductor and vice versa, they had rehearsed the timing very carefully.

The night of the concert arrived, and when the time came, the flute music floated in from offstage right on queue. Then all of a sudden, there was a loud, squeaky sound, followed by silence.

The conductor was furious! He couldn't wait to confront that flute player after the concert and chew him out. When the concert ended, the conductor searched out the flute player and went striding toward him, his face an angry scowl.

Seeing him approach, the flute player said, "Wait, wait, let me explain what happened! I was counting time, and I came in perfectly, didn't I?"

"Right," said the conductor.

"Well, right after I started to play, this monster of a guy came up behind me and said, 'Say, you fool, don't you know there's a concert going on out there?' He grabbed me and nearly choked me to death!"

The world can do the same kind of thing to us, even when we're doing good deeds. It will choke us almost to death and say, "Fool! There's a concert going on out there, and you're disturbing it!" Criticism is inevitable. But having the right reason for what we're doing can make all the difference in the world. It will give us strength and wisdom like Nehemiah's to stay focused and get the job done.

Other Good Goals

Although love is our primary, overriding motivation, other good goals are worthy of our pursuit as well. I'll describe three briefly.

For one, we know it is God's will for us to become more and more like His Son, Jesus Christ. "For those God foreknew he also predestined to be conformed to the likeness of his Son, that he might be the firstborn among many brothers" (Romans 8:29). God not only wants that, but He also works actively in our lives to bring it about, training us through discipline. As the writer to the Hebrews put it, "My son, do not make light of the Lord's discipline, and do not lose heart when he rebukes you, because the Lord disciplines those he loves, and he punishes everyone he accepts as a son" (Hebrews 12:5,6).

A good goal, then, is to work in cooperation with God as He develops Christlike character in us. We can accept His discipline, learn and grow, or we can resist and be frustrated. The choice is ours. Have you made it a goal to become more like Christ, to devote yourself to prayer, fellowship and the reading, study and memorization of God's Word so that He has something to work with as He forms Christ in you?

Another good purpose is to do something with our lives that will have lasting value, that will provide lasting benefit to others. Jesus said, "I chose you to go and bear fruit—fruit that will last" (John 15:16). The apostle Paul wrote, "For we are God's workmanship, created in Christ Jesus to do good works, which God prepared in advance for us to do" (Ephesians 2:10).

This kind of goal really lifts us above the mundane, doesn't it? So much of our time and energy seems tied up in material concerns like making a living, but Jesus told us not to worry about such things. Instead, He said, we should seek first the kingdom of God (Matthew 6:25-33). So let me ask: What are you doing these days? What's on your busy schedule for next week that will produce lasting, even eternal, value? If your honest answer is "not much," maybe you'll want to rethink how you're spending your life.

A third good purpose is to have something in your life that's worth dying for. Is anything that important to you? Jesus said, "Whoever wants to save his life will lose it, but whoever loses his life for me and for the gospel will save it. What good is it for a man to gain the whole world, yet forfeit his soul?" (Mark 8:35,36).

In response to the question "How do you want your life to end?", one of my students replied, "I don't know. I never really thought about it."

It's really sad to reach college age without ever having thought about that, isn't it? Yet, the majority of people who are much older, without realizing it, have never considered that question seriously. It's good to think about what you'd do if you had only six months to live, and it's also good to think about what you'd like to be remembered for when you're gone. What will people say was important to you?

Some people, sadly, will kill or die for money. Some will die for their loved ones. Many are willing to die for their country, and many more will die for a great cause like freedom. The greatest cause, of course, is the kingdom of God, and many people have died for their loyalty to Christ. Hebrews 11 tells us about just a few of them, and many others were martyred in places like communist China, the Soviet Union and Nazi Germany, to name just a few recent examples.

The Indians have a saying, and it's one we would all benefit from trying to apply: When you were born, you cried and the world rejoiced; live your life in such a manner that when you die, the world cries and you rejoice.

Don't Get Fragmented

I have always been intrigued by lion tamers, and I wondered for a long time why they carry a four-legged stool into the ring when they perform. They also carry a whip and a pistol, of course, and the reason for those is obvious. But why the stool? It wouldn't even slow down, much less stop, a charging lion.

It was William H. Hinson who told us the reason. The lion tamer holds the top of the stool and points the four legs at the lion because a lion will try to focus his eyes on all four legs at once. And when he does that, he becomes somewhat paralyzed and more tame. The fragmenting of his attention confuses him just a little and makes him less likely to act up or attack.

What a lesson on life! Most of us are so busy, involved in so many different things, that we've got a lot more than four legs pointing at us. As a result, our attention is fragmented. We get caught up in just trying to get by from day to day, and we lose sight of the larger issues in life. The great causes and important works God has for us are easily overlooked or endlessly postponed until some dreamed-of day when we'll have less responsibility and more free time.

We need a central reference point—Jesus Christ—and we need to stay focused on that point so that everything we do is in proper perspective. Questions raised earlier like "What would you do differently if you knew you had only six months to live?" and "What would you want to be remembered for?" will help you clarify your focus. I find that it also helps to remember that I'm never alone, never *really* by myself. The God who knows and cares about the intents of the heart is always with me—and you.

Years ago I heard a story told by a college football coach named Lou Little. He had a player on his team who wasn't very good, just a third-stringer. But the young man's father died, and just before the next game this young man went to the coach and asked, "Coach, is there any way I can start today against Fordham?"

Coach Little thought, "It's a big event, an emotional time for this young man. What could it hurt to let him start and be in there for just one play? Then I'll put the regular starter back in." So he told the young man, "Son, you know I can't let you play for long, but sure, you can start and go for a play or two."

Well, the young man went out and played the game of his life. From the opening kickoff, he was in on every play. He was all over the field, blocking and tackling like a monster man. Coach Little left him in the entire game, which they won, and that player was the key to their victory.

After the game, Coach Little met him in the locker room, put his arm around him, and said, "Son, I can't understand. You never played like that before. What in the world happened?"

"You know that my dad died," the young man answered.

"Sure, I know," the coach said.

"And you saw my dad and me when he visited the campus, and we walked around the grounds a lot, always arm in arm, with me leading him."

"Yes, I remember."

"Well, what you didn't know—very few people did—was that my father was blind. So today was the first time he ever saw me play."

If we can understand and remember that life is played out in a big stadium called earth and that our heavenly Father is watching us, it will make a tremendous difference in what we do and why we do it.

Chapter Reflection

When God sent Samuel to select a new king for Israel, He told him, "Do not look at his appearance or at the height of his stature. . . .for man looks at the outward appearance, but the Lord looks at the heart" (1 Samuel 16:7, NASB). David was selected to succeed Saul as king. Knowing that David would eventually let God down in some serious ways, why do you think God chose David?

Discussion Questions

1. In Matthew 15:8, Christ said, "This people honors me with their lips, but their heart is far from me." Why do our motives matter so much?

2. Do you agree that loving others gives life meaning? Is that the only thing that gives life meaning? If not, what else would you include?

3. How does the "love motivation" give our lives direction?

4. Anything one does can be criticized. How does a goal of love lift us above criticism?

3

Giving the Gift of Courtesy

Constant kindness can accomplish much. As the sun makes ice melt, kindness causes misunderstanding, mistrust, and hostility to evaporate.
(Albert Schweitzer)

Because I travel a lot, I often stay in motels and eat in restaurants. On one of my longer trips, I ate several times in a restaurant across from the motel, which had hostesses to seat customers. There were always plenty of customers because the food was so good, but I observed quite a difference in the atmosphere at noon and in the evening.

The noon hostess looked grumpy and treated people discourteously (maybe she was having a bad week). By her words and actions, she seemed to say to her customers, "Why are you here, making me work?" In response to her, the noon customers seemed more disgruntled, abrupt and cool toward her. There was no emotional warmth in the place at noontime.

On the other hand, in the evening there was a relaxed, congenial atmosphere in the place. The difference was easily discernable. The evening hostess was *friendly*. While customers waited for a table, she talked and joked with them and reassured them she would soon get them seated. Those people didn't seem to mind waiting much as they chatted with her. They clearly felt good about being there from the moment she greeted them so warmly. People tend to respond in like manner to the way they are treated.

The same is also true in the animal world, though to a different degree and over a longer period of time. Charlie Middleton was a mountain man who had a way with horses. Charlie lived alone and enjoyed the simple life. He lived with, and understood, nature. People would bring him their colts to be broken to the saddle. Charlie broke horses differently. And often, he'd spend hours with a horse, feeding it and just letting it get used to him. Gradually, he would begin to touch it, then rub its back, next put a sack on it and finally saddle it. The way Charlie broke horses, they never bucked.

I happened to be at his place one day when a man came to get some horses he had left with Charlie. The horses needed to be loaded into two trailers. The man who owned the horses grabbed the halter of one and started to lead him into his trailer. When they got to the wood ramp connecting the ground to the trailer bed, the animal stopped and pulled back. Clearly, he didn't want to go up that ramp. The owner jerked and pulled on the halter, trying to force the horse into the trailer. But the more he pulled and jerked, the more the horse pulled back. They had quite a battle, and the man became really frustrated and angry.

At the same time, Charlie gently led another horse to the trailer. Instead of trying to drag him up the ramp, though, Charlie stopped and let the horse look around, smell the ramp, and generally check out the surroundings for a minute. When the horse seemed satisfied that everything was all right, he walked up the ramp on his own. No struggle, no fuss, no need to strong-arm the horse.

When I saw the difference in the approaches of those two men and how the horses responded, my thought about Charlie was *What a master!* And what an example he also gave us of being courteous and patient with our children and others, allowing them time to understand things before we expect them to accept and act on them!

These two stories are not dramatic. You might even call them mundane, although they illustrate clearly the difference between courtesy and the lack of it. But courtesy, as simple as it is, is the oil of human kindness that makes all relationships—in the home, at work, in the church, in society—run smoothly. Wherever it's missing, a lot of friction inevitably appears. And it's my observation that in our nation, unfortunately, we're quickly losing our common courtesy. Still, 1 Corinthians 13:4 tells us, "Love is patient," and verse 5 tells us, "Love. . .is not rude."

Rudeness, the Sin That's In

Perhaps because I have been around young people so much, I have observed the lack of courtesy in them. I recall an incident from many years ago, when I was the basketball coach at a junior college. Because the student body was so small, it would be quickly apparent if a visible group like the basketball team stayed aloof from the rest of the students. So I encouraged the players to be an active part of campus life.

> *God didn't put people on this earth to be laughed at.*

One night they had a student talent show, and the players went as a group at my suggestion. A certain girl got up to do her number, and I'll admit her talent didn't show, but the way my players responded is seared into my memory. They laughed at the girl, right out loud, making no attempt to be discreet in their reaction. And the poor girl stopped and began to cry. And those fellows just kept on laughing.

No one enjoys a laugh more than I do, but God didn't put people on this earth to be laughed at. He put them here to be cared for. People with loving hearts know that, and they show courtesy to others, even if their best performance is not good.

I also remember traveling with the basketball team. After the game, even though I could get them into their hotel rooms by a certain time at night, they still wouldn't settle down and be quiet out of courtesy for the other guests. They'd still be noisy at one and two in the morning when other guests wanted to sleep.

"Guys, guys," I'd say, "remember there are other people here, and they want to sleep. Think about it!"

Yet, they never seemed to catch on. Why can't people think a little about how their actions affect others? I'm convinced most of us just don't think—totally don't think. And, as a result, we wind up being rude.

If it sounds like I'm picking on the younger generation, read on. The other day I was walking from a store to my car following a man who was retirement age. He had a paper cup in his hand, and as he went along, he just dropped that cup on the ground. There was no indication that he had looked for a trash can or that he felt a bit guilty about what he had done.

I picked up the cup to throw it away, but I also wanted to say to the man, "Hey, you dropped your cup! You didn't really mean to litter, did you?" Since I wasn't sure what his reaction would be, and I didn't want to create a scene, I kept my mouth shut. But I could not believe how rude and unthinking he had been.

Why can't we think about the impact of our words and actions on others? Why do our states have to spend millions of dollars each year just to clean litter from the highways? Why can't men lift the lid before they use the toilet? Why can't we let another driver merge in front of us in heavy traffic instead of cursing at anyone who tries? *We need to think lest we be rude.*

"Be kind and compassionate to one another," the apostle Paul commanded under the inspiration of the Holy Spirit in Ephesians 4:32. In Philippians 2:3,4 he added, "Do nothing out of selfish ambition or vain conceit, but in humility consider others better than yourselves. Each of you should look not only to your own interests, but also to the interests of others." That's God's will for everyone; yet, many Christians seem to think it's no big deal to ignore it.

The Key to Courtesy

The key to courtesy as a habit is simple: Imagine that your role and that of the other person were reversed, and think about how *you'd* want to be treated in that situation. In other words, *live by the golden rule.*

Over the last 100 years, literally tens (if not hundreds) of millions of words have been written about how to achieve success, happiness and joy. If you took all their words and put them in a winepress and tightened it down as hard as you could, the essence of truth that would remain is to *do unto others as you would have them do to you.* Or to rephrase the old cliche, you need to put yourself in the other person's shoes without getting athlete's foot.

> *Treat the other person as if the situation was reversed.*

So many of us seem unable to do this—maybe because it requires us to think before we act—but it's crucial. We have to work at it with the Lord's help, and we have to teach it to our children.

Here's a good way to test yourself on how well you're living by this principle. Suppose that starting tomorrow morning, you would be given one dollar for every kind word or deed you said or did for someone else—even if it was only a warm smile. However, you would have to give back 50 cents for every *unkind* word or deed. Now tell me: At the end of that first day, do you think you'd be richer or poorer than you were at the beginning? If you're not sure, why don't you try making an actual count? You'll probably be surprised at the results.

Another simple way to say all this is to say that we need to respect each other. As I mentioned earlier, God didn't make people to be abused but to be cared for, to be loved. And respect begins with recognizing that each person *is* the creation of God, made in His image, the object of His incredible love.

Think about it. If I don't respect you based on reverence for the God who made you, why should I be courteous to you? And therein lies the problem. In our public schools and in much of the rest of society, we've removed reverence for God. He has become irrelevant, even though most people still say they believe in Him. When was the last time you saw characters on a network T.V. show going to church? When was the last time you saw evangelical Christians portrayed in a positive light in any secular medium?

When you destroy reverence for God, you automatically destroy respect for others. If I don't love and revere the One who made you and want to please Him, why should I ever put your interests ahead of my own?

Scratch the Itch

When we see an opportunity to show kindness to someone else, we need to act on it right away. The longer we wait, the less likely it is that we'll ever follow through on our good intentions.

After you hear a good speaker, you may think, *Hey, I'll write that speaker a nice note for the great job.* But after you've had a couple of setbacks at work and two or three arguments with your spouse, a week later it doesn't seem quite appropriate to write the note. The opportunity has passed, and it never gets written.

So seize the chances to show kindness when they occur. Follow your impulses to be courteous. Don't dismiss them; act on them. The old Quaker prayer says it well: "I expect to pass this way but once. If, therefore, there be any kindness I can show or any good I can do for my fellow human beings, let me do it now. Let me not defer it nor neglect it, for I shall not pass this way again."

Once, when needing to mail a package, I waited in line in a

store that offers shipping services. The people in front of me at the counter had some ornaments and trinkets they wanted to mail, and they didn't have them ready. They weren't even in a box, just lying out on the counter. The young man working behind the counter could have gotten frustrated and sharp with those people very easily. After all, it was unreasonable for them to expect him to wrap their things, in addition to preparing them for shipping. Besides, he had at least one other customer waiting—me—and that could have added to the pressure he felt to be done with them as quickly as possible.

Instead, however, he was extremely kind and courteous with them. "No problem," he said. "I'll put them in a box for you and seal it up." He went the extra mile with a cheerful attitude, and he didn't even charge them for the added service. He took the opportunity to care for people who didn't deserve it.

I was so amazed that even though I was in a rush, I had to tell him, "Boy, you're really doing a great job! I appreciate what you're doing."

Little things like that young man's courtesy can make such a difference, often touching people we're not even aware of at the time. An incident I'll always remember took place 18 years ago, when John Stevens was president of the school where I teach, Abilene Christian University. I was the men's basketball coach at the time, and my office was in the coliseum, where we had chapel every day.

On one occasion, just before chapel was supposed to start, word came to Dr. Stevens that there was some need or emergency requiring his attention. So he walked into the secretary's office to use the phone, and I could see what was happening from my office, although he didn't know I was watching. As the president, he could have just reached for the phone and told her, "I need to use your phone." I think that's what I probably would have done in his place.

But not Dr. Stevens. He gently said to her, "I'm John Stevens. May I use your phone, please?" And when he finished his call, he thanked her for letting him use it.

It was such a simple demonstration of courtesy; yet, it impressed me tremendously. He had every right to be demanding, but instead he was kind. A loving heart doesn't just do big, grand things for other people. It gives the gift of courtesy in a hundred different ways, day in and day out.

> *Kindness and courtesy are more important than laws.*

When you stop to think about it, the truth is that kindness and courtesy are more important than our laws. The law only touches us every now and then, just here and there. And it's easily ignored when there's no police officer around to enforce it. But kindness and courtesy affect us many times every day—every time we interact with another person. Their presence or absence reflect the kind of people we are, especially when we're in any sort of difficult situation. Are we still fair and polite then, considering others' feelings?

The Perfect Example

Not surprisingly, Jesus is the perfect example of kindness and courtesy. He could be hard on hypocrites, all right, but He was kind to those who had made a lot of mistakes and admitted it, as well as to those who were weak.

In Mark 10:13-16, people were bringing their children to Jesus, just to have Him touch them. However, His disciples apparently considered the children a nuisance, and they wanted to send them away. But Jesus got indignant at that, and He said, "Let the little children come to me, and do not hinder them, for the kingdom of God belongs to such as these" (v. 14). As the story ends, Jesus was taking them in His arms and blessing them.

In the very next section of Mark 10 (vv. 17-22), Jesus encountered a rich young ruler who had a spiritual question, and again He was exceedingly kind. Verse 21 tells us, "Jesus looked at him and loved him." He took his question seriously and treated him with respect.

Stop and think for a minute about how you would have felt toward someone who was young, rich and a ruler. Our natural human tendency is to envy or resent a person who's younger and making a lot more money. Could you have been kind and courteous to that young man, or would you have been cynical or bitter?

Jesus' kindness really shows in the way He handled interruptions. I'm always amazed at how His life seemed to be a series of interruptions; yet, He was unfailingly courteous. He was busy teaching when the parents brought their children to Him. He was on His way to someplace else when the rich young ruler asked for His attention.

Jesus was accusingly called "a friend of sinners" because He kindly took meals with sinners like Zacchaeus, the corrupt tax collector, when no one else would. He showed compassion to the woman caught in adultery and the Samaritan woman at the well. He lovingly healed the sick, cast demons out of the possessed and raised the dead to life again. On two occasions, He miraculously fed crowds of people because, in part, they had been following Him for days and were hungry, and He didn't want to send them away in that condition.

Our assignment as His modern disciples is to show the same care to those in our world—to imitate Him. There's absolutely no limit to this kindness. Jesus even told us to treat our enemies well (Matthew 5:43-48). Why? Because in doing so, we'll be following the example of our Father in heaven: "But God demonstrates his own love for us in this: While we were still sinners, Christ died for us" (Romans 5:8).

We'll also be serving Jesus as we show kindness to those who are in any kind of need (Matthew 25:31-46). I came across a poem some time ago that expresses this beautifully:

Unawares

They said: "The Master is coming
   To honor the town today,
And none can tell at whose house or home
   The Master will choose to stay."
And I thought, while my heart beat wildly,
   What if He should come to mine?
How would I strive to entertain
   And honor the guest divine!

And straight I turned to toiling
   To make my home more neat;
I swept and polished and garnished,
   And decked it with blossoms sweet.
I was troubled for fear the Master
   Might come ere my task was done,
And I hastened and worked the faster,
   And watched the hurrying sun.

But right in the midst of my duties,
   A woman came to my door;
She had come to tell me her sorrows,
   And my comfort and aid to implore.
And I said: "I cannot listen
   Nor help you any today;
I have greater things to attend to."
   And the pleader turned away.

But soon there came another—
   A cripple, thin, pale and gray;
And said: "Oh, let me stop and rest
   A while in your home, I pray!
I have traveled far since morning,
   I am hungry and faint and weak.
My heart is full of misery,
   And comfort and help I seek."

And I said: "I am grieved and sorry,
   But I cannot help you today;
I look for a great and noble guest."
   And the cripple went away.

And the day wore onward swiftly,
   And my task was nearly done,
And a prayer was ever in my heart,
   That the Master to me might come.

And I thought I would spring to meet Him,
   And serve Him with utmost care,
When a little child stood by me
   With a face so sweet and fair;
Sweet, but with marks of teardrops,
   And his clothes were tattered and old.
A finger was bruised and bleeding,
   And his little bare feet were cold.

And I said: "I am sorry for you;
   You're sorely in need of care;
But I cannot stop to give it;
   You must hasten otherwhere."
And at the words a shadow
   Swept o'er his blue-veined brow;
"Someone will feed and clothe you, dear,
   But I am too busy now."

At last the day was ended,
   And my toil was over and done;
My house was swept and garnished,
   And I watched in the dusk alone;
Watched, but no footfall sounded,
   No one paused at my gate,
No one entered my cottage door.
   I could only pray and wait.

I waited till night had deepened,
   And the Master had not come.
"He has entered some other door," I cried,
   "And gladdened some other home!
My labor has been for nothing!"
   And I bowed my head and wept;
My heart was sore with longing,
   Yet, in spite of all, I slept.

Then the Master stood before me,
   And His face was grave and fair.

> "Three times today I came to your door
> And craved your pity and care;
> Three times you sent Me onward,
> Unhelped and uncomforted;
> And the blessing you might have had was lost,
> And your chance to serve has fled."
>
> "O Lord, dear Lord, forgive me!
> How could I know it was Thee?"
> My very soul was shamed and bowed
> In the depths of humility.
> And He said: "Thy sin is pardoned,
> But the blessing is lost to thee;
> For comforting not the least of Mine,
> Ye have failed to comfort Me."
>
> —Author Unknown

Let me close with a story that's maybe an extreme example of imitating Christ in showing kindness; yet, I think it makes an important point. The story comes from Brennan Manning in his book *The Signature of Jesus*.

And old Indian man used to meditate every morning on the bank of the Ganges River. One day, when he finished meditating, he saw a scorpion floating helplessly on the water, close to drowning. As the scorpion came near, the old man reached out to rescue it. When he touched it, however, the scorpion stung him.

Instantly, the man withdrew his hand. But soon he tried to save the scorpion again. This time it stung him so severely with its poisonous tail that his hand began to swell and bleed, and his face contorted with pain.

At that point, a bystander saw what was happening and said, "Hey, stupid old man, what's wrong with you? Only a fool would risk his life for such an ugly, evil creature. Don't you know you could kill yourself trying to save an ungrateful scorpion?"

Looking the bystander straight in the eye, the old man replied, "My friend, just because it's the scorpion's nature to sting does not change my nature to save."

Jesus' nature was to show courtesy and kindness to others. Therefore, that's also the nature of a loving human heart.

Chapter Reflection

Scripture has much to say about relationships between both friends and enemies. Read Romans 12:10, Ephesians 4:32, 1 Peter 4:9 and Philippians 2:3,4. What are the implications of these verses for Christians?

Discussion Questions

1. How is being courteous a habit of love? Explain.
2. Is the golden rule, "Do unto others as you would have others do unto you," a biblical principle? Explain.
3. If Christians are supposed to be courteous, is being discourteous a sin? Give some specific examples of discourtesies that are prevalent today.
4. What does discourtesy say about the individual who is discourteous and about his attitude toward the object of his discourtesy?

4

Rejoicing, Not Resentful

Love looks through a telescope; envy, through a microscope.
(Josh Billings)

There were two young men who lived near each other and worked very hard at their respective jobs. The older of them was a farmer, and the younger owned sheep. They were brothers. Both men were devout people who regularly worshiped God. They knew Him well and recognized His authority over their lives.

One of these brothers not only sought to worship God, but he was careful to do it in just the way God had told them He wanted. This was the younger brother, and part of his proper worship was offering to the Lord a sacrifice of the firstborn lamb from his flocks.

The older brother, however, had his own ideas about how to worship God. Showing a rebellious streak, he decided that he would not go to his brother to get a lamb to sacrifice. Instead, he would offer God some of the produce he had grown in his fields.

Not surprisingly, the Lord was pleased with the man who had obeyed His instructions, and with his sacrifice, and He was not pleased with the farmer and his offering. He expressed this to the brothers.

How did the unfavored brother react? Did he repent of his willfulness and commit himself to worshiping properly? Did he praise his younger brother for his faithfulness to God? In short, did he learn anything?

No, unfortunately, he didn't do any of those things. Instead, he envied his brother's favor in God's eyes. The dictionary says envy is "painful or resentful awareness of an advantage enjoyed by another, joined with a desire to possess the same advantage." That's the way the older brother felt. He was painfully aware of the difference in how God viewed him and his brother, and he resented the favor his brother enjoyed.

That envy in turn gave birth to anger, which showed clearly on the young man's face. God knew this, and He spoke to him. "If you do what is right," He said, "will you not be accepted?" And then God gave him this warning: "If you do not do what is right, sin is crouching at your door; it desires to have you, but you must master it."

Even then, however, the young man would not learn and repent. His envy-fueled anger continued to grow until it became a terrible thing. Finally, his resentment toward his brother led him to lure his brother into a deserted field, and there he murdered him, his own flesh and blood.

And so the story of Cain and Abel, from Genesis 4—the first children born to the human race—tells us that envy was one of the first sins committed by our forefathers. Their story also shows that sibling rivalry has been around since the beginning!

Envy is incredibly destructive. It *can* do great harm to others—Abel was killed—but it *always* hurts the one who harbors it. As a basketball coach, I watched players destroy their own careers because they were jealous of other players who were getting more attention. I learned that in practice, I couldn't have the number-six player, the first guy off the bench, scrimmage against the five starters, because the rivalry was simply too intense. It would start a cycle of envy rolling that would put an edge on the entire practice.

Dwight L. Moody once told a fable about an eagle that was

envious of a fellow eagle that could fly better and higher. One day, the envious eagle saw a hunter with a bow and arrow. The eagle said to the sportsman, "I wish you would bring down that soaring eagle up there."

"I would," the man said, "if you'd give me some feathers for this arrow so it will fly farther and straighter."

So the jealous eagle pulled out his own feathers and gave them to the hunter, who put them on his arrow. But his shot still fell short of the high-flying eagle.

That led the envious eagle to pull out another feather and then another for the man's arrows, until finally he had pulled out so many that the bird couldn't fly. The hunter then took advantage of the situation, turning around and killing the now-helpless bird.

Have you ever noticed how many fables deal with envy? It's the story of mankind without love, and it's true that jealousy usually backfires. A classic biblical example comes from the book of Esther, where the evil Haman learned his lesson the hard way.

He had been honored by his master, the Persian King Xerxes, who ordered all the palace staff to kneel and honor Haman whenever he passed by. All of them obeyed except Mordecai, a Jew. Haman resented Mordecai's disrespect so much that he became enraged and plotted to destroy not just Mordecai, but the entire Jewish race.

Before Haman could carry out his plot, however, the king was reminded of how Mordecai had once saved his life. Queen Esther also spoke up courageously to expose Haman's plot. And the end result was that Haman was hanged on the same gallows he had built to execute Mordecai.

In contrast, 1 Corinthians 13:4 tells us that "love . . . does not envy." A loving heart isn't pained when others do well or find favor. It doesn't resent their success or happiness. And it certainly doesn't get angry about what others have. Instead, it can rejoice with those who are rejoicing (Romans 12:15).

The Bible further tells us, "A heart at peace gives life to the body, but envy rots the bones" (Proverbs 14:30). We saw the truth of the following verse in the stories of Cain and Haman: "For where you have envy and selfish ambition, there you find disorder and every evil practice" (James 3:16).

It's not surprising, then, that God's Word commands in 1 Peter 2:1, "Therefore, rid yourselves of all malice and all deceit, hypocrisy, *envy*, and slander of every kind" (emphasis added). But it's not enough just to try to get rid of something evil. We have to replace it with something good—something far better, in fact.

That something, the opposite of envy and the reason a loving heart can rejoice, is thankfulness. A loving heart is a thankful heart—thankful for life, for God's grace, for friends and family, for the beauty of the world, for freedom and for a host of other things. It's filled with gratitude to God for all His blessings rather than with resentment for what it doesn't have.

A Matter of Focus

When you boil it down, whether we're envious or thankful is simply a matter of focus. It's a question of what we *choose* to think about and fill our minds with.

> *Envious or thankful? It's simply a matter of focus!*

You see, we all have problems. We all want things we don't have. Even the people whose lives seem most "together" and the people with the biggest bank accounts could give you a list of woes and wants if you asked. Remember the quote from Jack Lemmon in chapter 2 that money and fame don't end your problems—they just bring you a new set of troubles.

On the other hand, even people going through tough times have a lot of things for which they can be thankful if they choose to be, the kinds of things I mentioned just above. We're all so richly blessed. We fail to think we're blessed most of the time, however, but it's not because we haven't been blessed. Instead, it's because we take so many of our blessings for granted.

What we need to do, then, is look for the good in life; look for those things for which we can be genuinely thankful. It's a basic fact of life that we find what we look for, whether it's positive or negative, something to be envious about or something to be thankful for. And what we allow our minds to dwell on shapes our attitudes and, sooner or later, our words and actions.

One of the best examples of someone who knows how to look for the good in life is the preacher who bravely spoke one Sunday about giving and supporting the church. His congregation was a rather stingy group of people. But after the sermon, he passed his hat to take up a collection anyway.

When the hat had made its way to all the people and back to the preacher, he optimistically turned it over to see what would fall out. He shook it, but nothing came out. Finally, he said, "Let's pray." And then he thanked the Lord that he got his hat back!

Deciding to look for the good, to be thankful and to rejoice with those who rejoice isn't a one-time thing. We have to keep at it—work at it—every day. Appreciating what we have is like an insurance policy—we have to keep it renewed or it runs out. It's not in our fallen human nature to be positive. As Cain made so clear, it's our human nature to be negative, envious, angry and even murderous. So we work each day at developing the kind of Christlike love described in 1 Corinthians 13.

Just what triggers envy? It comes when we compare ourselves in some way to someone else and don't like what we see. Cain compared himself and his standing with God to Abel and his standing, and the end result was murdering his brother. One man compares his house or his car to his neighbor's, and the result is envy and covetousness. One student compares his test score to that of the class genius, and the result is envy and a temptation to cheat the next time.

Another biblical example is found in Matthew 20, in which

Rejoicing, Not Resentful

Jesus tells the parable of the workers in the vineyard. A landowner went out early in the morning, Jesus said, and hired some men to work in his vineyard. They agreed to work all day for one denarius, which was a common day's pay in that time and place.

The landowner also went out and hired men at about nine in the morning, at noon and again at three in the afternoon. All agreed to work for the rest of the day for one denarius. Finally, the owner went out at about five in the afternoon, just one hour before quitting time, and hired still more men to work for the rest of the day.

When evening, or 6:00, rolled around, the owner had his foreman call the workers in and pay them their wages, beginning with those hired last. Those last workers each received a denarius. When those hired first saw it, they got excited. "If he's being so generous with those men," they reasoned among themselves, "surely he'll be even more generous with us, since we worked all day in the hot sun!"

But when those men got to the foreman, each of them also received just one denarius. Their instant reaction was negative: They were envious of the men who had worked only one hour and got the same pay as they did. They were angry at the landowner, feeling he should pay them more because they worked longer.

Here again, envy led to anger as the all-day workers compared their wages to those of the one-hour workers and resented what they saw. They didn't take any satisfaction in having done an honest day's work. They didn't appreciate the fact that because the landowner had given them work for the day and paid them a fair wage, they would be able to feed their families that night. They ignored the wage agreement they had made with the landowner when they were hired. And they couldn't rejoice with the short-term workers in their good fortune.

To put it simply, there was no love in their hearts, only envy and anger.

Comparing ourselves to others will always lead to envy, disappointment, frustration and, eventually, anger. Why? Because someone else will always have more or better or be smarter, better looking or more highly honored. There's just no way to win the comparison game.

I like the way a writer named Benjamin Stein put it in a recent *Reader's Digest* article titled "How to Live Another Year":

> *Comparing leads to envy, envy leads to disappointment.*

[Envy] is a poison just like strychnine. If you want to hurt yourself, think of all the people who have more money or power than you do. But if you want to live another year, think of what you have that you don't deserve, and for which you should be prostrate with gratitude. I do not in any sense deserve the good fortune of being an American, of having such a wonderful family, of being able to do the interesting work I do. If I concentrate on that, I believe I will live.

The Way to Happiness

The way to happiness, then, is to focus continually on the blessings we have instead of on whatever it is that someone else has. William Law, a great religious writer of yesteryear, said it well:

If anyone could tell you the shortest, surest way to all happiness and all perfection, he must tell you to thank and praise God for everything that happens to you. For it is sure that whatever seeming calamity happens to you, if you thank and praise God for it, you turn it into a blessing. Could you therefore work miracles? You could not do more for yourself than by this thankful spirit, for it turns all that it touches into happiness.

The book of James tells us we should even consider it joy when we encounter trials, knowing they help us to grow in Christlikeness (James 1:2-4). Hebrews 12:1-13 gives us the same message. Gratitude produces happiness; ingratitude produces unhappiness. It couldn't be simpler.

I'm reminded of a wealthy couple who made the news a while back. They and their small children were sailing on the ocean on their 35 foot sloop when they ran into a fierce storm. Their boat capsized, and all their goods onboard were lost. The family had to be pulled out of the water by a rescue team.

Later, when the couple were interviewed by a reporter, the woman kept saying over and over, "We've lost everything! Everything was in that sailboat—all our money, our clothes, our possessions—and the yacht wasn't insured! We've lost everything!"

It's so easy to think that way, isn't it? We focus on the things we own and how that compares to what others have, and we're unhappy. And if we lose our possessions, we're even more unhappy. Yet, the woman and her husband and children had been saved from drowning, and none of them was much the worse for the wear. So the truth is that they had lost *nothing* of real, lasting value—nothing that couldn't be replaced. Isn't it better to realize how blessed we are and be grateful for that?

My wife, Bobbie, once made a statement after we'd lost some money in a business deal, and it has stayed with me because it's so simple yet so profound. "If you can count your losses in money," she said, "you haven't lost much." How very true that is! And if we can keep it in mind, we'll have a far easier time being grateful to God.

Bobbie's statement brings us to another important point, which is that we need people with a thankful attitude around us to give us the right, encouraging example. We need to be reminded constantly of how good we have it. And there's power in examples.

I've seen the power of example many times in my college classes. When the students tell a little of their personal history, if the first one to speak is open, spontaneous and really giving, the others follow suit, and the sharing becomes really rich and deep. But if the one leading off is flighty, superficial or doesn't take the assignment seriously, it's difficult to ever get the discussion on a serious, helpful track.

Because examples are so powerful, we need to search out people who have a grateful, appreciative attitude and spend time with them. Their gratitude will spread to us, feeding our spirits positively instead of with the negativism that's so common.

One such example that meant a lot to me and many others was a student by the name of Willie Mickna. Willie had been a star athlete, an outstanding quarterback on his high school football team. He was ready to go to a major college on a full scholarship. Then he was involved in a serious car accident, and his legs were injured. The doctor said Willie would never walk again. By the time he got to my class, however, Willie was walking, but very slowly. He had made an excellent recovery, although he certainly was not the great athlete he had formerly been.

One of the subjects we cover in my class is how to grow in self-confidence. Among some 15 suggestions for growth, one I always make is that the students learn to walk faster, to put some excitement and energy into their lives—to get a little get-up-and-go in their get-along.

After offering these suggestions in Willie's class, I went around the room and asked each student which one they most needed to work on. When I got to Willie, he said, "Walk faster."

Everyone got a good chuckle out of that, but we also got a wonderful example of a healthy, positive attitude. Willie wasn't envious of the rest of us who could move easily and without pain. He wasn't bitter toward God, either. Instead, he was grateful for his life, he enjoyed it immensely, and he helped the rest of us to appreciate life more. He is the kind of person others like to be around, and with good reason.

What God Expects

First Corinthians 13:4 tells us that loving hearts don't envy. I've given several reasons why I believe that's the case, but there's one more I need to mention, and it's probably the most important. Namely, the Bible makes it clear that God *expects*

His people to be grateful for His blessings rather than envious of anyone else.

When we stop to think of all the Lord has done for us and given us, starting with the salvation earned by His precious, sinless Son on the cross, our hearts should be filled with gratitude. To love Him and praise Him and appreciate His goodness should be our daily response to His great love.

God's reasonable desire for our thanks can be seen throughout the Bible, but let me draw your attention to just two places where it can be seen clearly.

In Deuteronomy 6, God was preparing the people of Israel to enter and conquer the land of Canaan and make it their own. And beginning in verse 10, He told them, "When the Lord your God brings you into the land he swore to your fathers, to Abraham, Isaac and Jacob, to give you—a land with large, flourishing cities you did not build, houses filled with all kinds of good things you did not provide, wells you did not dig, and vineyards and olive groves you did not plant." In other words, they would be blessed with great prosperity.

Then, when all that happened, "Be careful that you do not forget the Lord, who brought you out of Egypt, out of the land of slavery" (v. 12). Likewise in 8:10,11, God warned, "When you have eaten and are satisfied, praise the Lord your God for the good land he has given you. Be careful that you do not forget the Lord your God."

The Lord knows that when things are going well for us, we tend to feel self-sufficient and to forget where our blessings come from. We forget to be grateful. So He cautioned the Israelites, and us through them, not to forget.

In Luke 17:11-19, we have the story of Jesus' healing 10 lepers on the border between Galilee and Samaria. They begged for Him to take pity and heal them, and He did so. Then, He instructed them to go show themselves to the priests and be certified as "clean," as the law of Moses required.

Afterward, only one of the 10 was grateful enough to come back, find Jesus and express thanks for His healing. That one was a Samaritan, not a Jew like Jesus. And Christ asked him,

"Were not all ten cleansed? Where are the other nine? Was no one found to return and give praise to God except this foreigner?"

Obviously, all 10 former lepers had plenty of reason to seek out the Lord and thank Him, and Jesus indicated that's exactly what they should have done. It was a reasonable expectation for them, and it's entirely reasonable for us, as well.

We know that a thankful, nonenvious attitude is the surest way to happiness. We see once again that God has the greatest loving heart of all because what He asks of us is the very thing that's also best for us. He has our good in mind always. He knows how we're made (He made us!), He knows what we need, He loves us forever and He blesses us abundantly and continually.

When we keep all that in mind, we realize there's no reason to compare ourselves to others. God has given each of us intrinsic worth that we don't have to earn. His willingness to send Jesus to die to save us while we were still sinners in rebellion against Him (Romans 5:8) establishes that fact beyond a shadow of a doubt. We don't need to prove we're more worthy than someone else.

Most of my life, I thought I had to blow out another person's candle to make my own burn brighter. But when I recall that I'm loved with an everlasting love, that I'm a child of the living God and worth the life of Jesus to redeem, then I can begin to love others without feeling jealous and envious of them.

In light of all that, what place does envy have in our lives? How can we neglect to be grateful? God help us to remember to always be grateful. And if we do, we will be lifted to a plane of joy and fellowship with Him that few people have ever reached.

Chapter Reflection

Beginning with Cain and Abel, envy has been a problem for mankind. Scriptures list envy along with wickedness, greed, evil, murder, strife, deceit, malice, gossip, hate, deception, abusive language, lust, hypocrisy and evil suspicions (1 Peter 2:1, Romans 1:29, 1 Timothy 6:4 and Titus 3:3).

Discussion Questions

1. How would you define envy?
2. List some situations in which we might be tempted to envy.
3. What is the basis of envy? Why is envy so contradictory to being Christlike?
4. Read Hebrews 12:28 and Colossians 2:7. Why should we be grateful and not envious?
5. Discuss the meaning of Bobbie's quote "If you can count your losses in money, you haven't lost much."

5
Showing True Humility

Man was created on the sixth day so that he could not be boastful, since he came after the flea in the order of creation.

(Haggadah)

Tom Brokaw, anchorman on "NBC Nightly News," is very well known and highly paid. He told the following story of a time when he was humbled in a humorous way. He had just been promoted to be co-host of "The Today Show," NBC's morning news and information program. He said he thought he had reached the pinnacle of success, and he was feeling pretty good about himself—until—one day when he was in a store, he noticed that a man kept watching him. "Well, that's the price you pay for celebrity," he thought. Finally, the man came over, pointed at Brokaw and said, "You're Tom Brokaw, aren't you?"

Brokaw smiled, stood a little straighter, and answered, "Yes, that's right."

"You used to do the morning news back on KMTV in Omaha, Neb., didn't you?"

"Yes, you're right again," Brokaw said, really enjoying the notoriety now.

"I'd have spotted you in a minute, man," the fellow said with a smile. Then he got a puzzled look on his face and added, "Whatever happened to you, anyhow?"

Life has a way of keeping us humble, doesn't it? But the fact is that loving hearts make a habit of showing true humility. Rather than getting caught up in the prideful egotism that's a hallmark of our human nature, they routinely demonstrate the same humility modeled by the Lord Jesus Christ.

What Humility Is

What exactly is humility? It's commonly misunderstood and, unfortunately, not overly exemplified. So let's examine this quality more closely.

First, humility means being quiet about yourself. It means not blowing your own horn. It's so easy to brag in the effort to feel important. Personally, I find it difficult to do a good deed and keep it a secret. Occasionally, as I'm walking across our college campus, I'll stop and pick up some litter, and I confess that I'd like for someone to see me and give me a verbal pat on the back.

Are you like that? Can you relate to my simple example? Most of us, if we're honest, would have to answer in the affirmative.

As a public speaker, I'm in front of large groups of people quite often. And often I receive compliments on the presentation. Having been a member of the National Speaker's Association, I am aware that speakers are taught to project a confident, in-charge kind of image. But it's difficult to project that image and at the same time project humility. It's not always easy for me to show humility, but as everyone who wants to have a loving heart, I work at it.

Not tooting our own horns is made easier if we think back to Matthew 6 (a passage we looked at in chapter 2), where Jesus warns us about doing good things for the wrong reasons. That will help us to keep our motives and our deeds in perspective.

Second, humility means we don't look "down" on others—in fact, we do just the opposite. The apostle Paul said in Philippians 2:3,4, "Do nothing out of selfish ambition or vain conceit, but in humility consider others better than yourselves. Each of you should look not only to your own interests, but also to the interests of others."

If that's not clear enough, Jesus made the same point unmistakably in Luke 18:9-14:

To some who were confident of their own righteousness [i.e., proud] and looked down on everybody else, Jesus told this parable: "Two men went up to the temple to pray, one a Pharisee and the other a tax collector. The Pharisee stood up and prayed about himself; 'God, I thank you that I am not like all other men—robbers, evildoers, adulterers—or even like this tax collector. I fast twice a week and give a tenth of all I get.'

"But the tax collector stood at a distance. He would not even look up to heaven, but beat his breast and said, 'God, have mercy on me, a sinner.'

"I tell you that this man, rather than the other, went home justified before God. For everyone who exalts himself will be humbled, and he who humbles himself will be exalted."

M.L. Bowen put it this way: "You should have enough education so you won't have to look up to people, and then more education so you'll be wise enough not to look down on people."

We should *not* be like the man whose wife slipped into bed beside him and said, "Lord, I'm tired."

He turned and whispered in her ear, "You can call me Jack in private."

In a more serious vein, if we make a habit of looking down on others, we easily slip into a judgmental, holier-than-thou attitude. To help us guard against that, we would all benefit from a regular reading of James 4:11,12: "Brothers, do not slander one another. Anyone who speaks against his brother or judges him, speaks against the law and judges it. When you judge the law, you are not keeping it, but sitting in judgment on it. There is only one Lawgiver and Judge, the one who is able to save and destroy. But you—who are you to judge your neighbor?"

Then we should pray sincerely, "Lord, am I guilty of this in any way today? If so, show me and forgive me and cleanse me, I pray."

Third, humility means letting others shine—not playing the status game. It's so difficult to let someone else have the spotlight, isn't it? But the loving heart is content to let others bask in the applause.

A little writing titled "A Friend" captures this side of humility:

> A friend—his love for you is tops when you're at the bottom. He looks up to you when the rest of the world is looking down on you. He lets you step on his toes to help you get back on your feet. He shows you the meaning of true friendship and not the meaninglessness of it. He shoots straight for you, not at you. He knows the most about your faults, and cares the least. And when you're wrong he tells you, not the rest of the world.
>
> He doesn't complain when you neglect him, but beefs when you neglect yourself. And when you flop he never splits with you, except what he has. And when you achieve success, he wants nothing more than to know about it. He lets you worry him more than his enemies. He's the best press agent, and he doesn't have to be paid to boost you.
>
> His friendship is the kind you won't lose, even when you deserve to. He stands behind you when you're taking bows and beside you when you're taking boos. No greater love has a man than to lay down his life for his friend.
>
> —Author Unknown

Most people are too timid to grab for attention openly. Instead, sometimes we follow the world in playing the status game, seeking attention in a subtler way. We're more concerned about the brand names on the things we buy than we are about their quality or value—about the status level of our cars than about having the most suitable transportation to meet our needs.

Somehow, I don't think Jesus would have considered designer jeans or little alligators on his shirts a big deal. He wouldn't have thought any more (or less) of a person driving a Mercedes than He would of a person driving a Chevrolet. If

I had been making the entry into Jerusalem, I probably would have asked for the biggest, finest, whitest, grandest stallion, but Jesus was content to ride in on a donkey. Today, that would be like driving into town in a '56 Studebaker!

I read a good definition of egotism: It's the anesthetic that dulls the pain of stupidity. Nothing is as difficult to do as getting down off your high horse gracefully, but loving hearts seldom get on high horses.

An old man was the organist in a great cathedral. His music was inspiring. But on one particular Sunday, it was sadder than usual. After the service, someone asked him about it.

"I've been playing the organ here for a long time," he said, "but I'm going to be replaced by a young man today. Playing here has been my work and my life." Clearly, he was pained by the idea of having to let go and let someone else shine in his place.

> *Humility wants others to shine.*

As the day came to a close, he noticed the new organist at the back of the cathedral. Reluctantly, the old man took the key, locked the organ and walked back to the younger man. As he walked, he noticed that the setting sun, as it came through the stained-glass windows, was somehow more beautiful than he'd ever seen it before.

At the young man's request, he slowly handed him the organ key. The younger man quickly walked to the instrument, sat down and then slowly, as if he might break it, opened the keyboard, positioned his hands and began to play. The old man sat down in the back to listen.

The elderly organist knew he had always played beautifully. But shortly after the new man began to play, he realized he was in the presence of sheer genius. The music he heard was beyond what he ever could have performed, even in his prime. It was joyful; it was enthralling.

Thus did the world hear for the first time the brilliance of Johann Sebastian Bach.

Another person who was watching all this asked the old man, "Why are you so happy?"

He responded, "Oh, you see, I'm happy because I've given the master the key."

That's humility—not promoting self but letting another shine.

Some Hard Truths

The experience of the old organist illustrates a truth that many of us have a difficult time swallowing. Namely, *no one* of us is indispensable, no matter how much we might like to think we are.

The president of a large university showed a good grasp of this part of humility when he told a colleague, "Be kind to your A and B students, because some day they may return to your campus and be your professors. But be *extremely* kind to your C students, because one day one of them will return and build you a $2 million science lab."

Winston Churchill showed he understood, too. He was stopped one day by a woman who said, "Doesn't it thrill you, Mr. Churchill, to know that every time you speak, the hall is packed to overflowing?"

"It is quite flattering," Churchill responded. "But whenever I feel that way, I always remember that if, instead of giving a political speech, I was being hanged, the crowd would be twice as big."

Harry Truman, when he took over the Oval Office after the death of Franklin Roosevelt, was fed a similar dose of humility by Speaker of the House Sam Rayburn. Rayburn, a blunt Texan, told him, "From here on out, you're going to be surrounded by a lot of people. They're going to try to build a wall around you and cut you off from any ideas other than theirs. And they're going to tell you often how great a man you are. But Harry, you and I both know you ain't."

I hate to be the bearer of bad news, but let me give you an

idea of just how important you are: The size of your funeral is going to be determined by the weather. If it rains that day, they will stay home.

I know what will happen when I die. Folks will be sitting around playing a game with their friends; they will hear about my death and say, "That's too bad about Willard, isn't it?" " Whose turn is it?" That'll be about it. (I *am* trying to get six good friends before that time comes, though, to carry the box. It would be bad if one handle was open and the coffin was leaning as they carried me out of the church building!)

A little poem sums up this truth:

> Sometimes when you're feeling important,
> And sometimes when your ego is in full bloom,
> And sometimes when you take it for granted
> That you're the best qualified in the room,
>
> Sometimes when you feel that your going,
> That your going would leave an unfilled hole,
> Just follow these simple instructions
> And see how they humble your soul:
>
> Take a bucket, and fill it with water,
> And put your hand in up to your wrist.
> Pull it out, and the hole that's remaining
> Is the size of how much you'll be missed!
>
> You may splash all you please as you enter,
> And you can stir up the water galore,
> But stop and you'll find in a minute
> It looks quite as it did before.
>
> Now the moral of this quaint example
> Is just do the best that you can.
> Be grateful for your talents,
> But remember there's no indispensable man [or woman].
> —Author Unknown

Another hard truth is that life is designed to keep us humble, if we'll allow it. Our circumstances and problems and the situations that are beyond our control are meant to keep us from growing big heads.

Showing True Humility

A lady who worked in a coffee shop went to take her afternoon break. She had a small bag of cookies to eat and a magazine to read, both in her purse. All the seats in the shop were taken, however, except for one at a table where a man was already sitting, quietly reading the paper.

So the woman sat down without disturbing him, took out her magazine, and began to read. In a little bit, she reached out for one of her cookies on the table. To her surprise, the man did the same thing. She couldn't believe it! It made her a little angry, but she kept still and just went back to her reading.

A short time later, the same thing happened again. She took a cookie, and so did the man. She glared at him as if to say, "How dare you!" But he simply smiled and went back to his reading.

Before long, her coffee break was over, and she got up and walked away, looking angrily at the man as she passed him. Then it happened. She opened her purse to put away her magazine—and there was her bag of cookies, still unopened! She had been eating the man's cookies!

Yes, life has a way of keeping us humble.

A second hard truth is that pride is a sin. It's no small matter to God whether we're humble or proud. We read in Proverbs 21:4, "Haughty eyes and a proud heart, the lamp of the wicked, are sin!" Proverbs 16:5 tells us, "The Lord detests all the proud of heart." In Proverbs 8:13, wisdom says, "I hate pride and arrogance."

In the New Testament, Paul said that in the last days "people will be lovers of themselves, lovers of money, boastful, proud" and a bunch of other evil things (2 Timothy 3:2). And the apostle John wrote, "For everything in the world—the cravings of sinful man, the lust of his eyes and the boasting of what he has and does—comes not from the Father but from the world" (1 John 2:16).

Augustine said pride is the greatest sin of all because it exalts us and displaces God. In the same vein, C.S. Lewis called pride the complete anti-God state of mind.

You know, you can get to the point where you even become

proud of your humility. Did you hear about the guy who was awarded a badge in honor of his humility? He didn't get to keep his humility badge, though. They took it back because he *wore* it.

The world today looks down on humility as a weakness. It doesn't fit the American success formula. But the loving, humble heart has learned to obey God and so has a freedom and a joy the world will never understand. No force on earth can stand up to that kind of humility and submission.

A third hard truth follows all too logically after the last one: Pride is destructive. It's socially destructive because no one wants to be around a proud person, and also because the proud person looks down on others, which comes across loud and clear. It's spiritually destructive because it tempts us to think we can get along just fine without God.

Pride can also destroy us by bringing God's wrath down upon us. Previously quoted, the first part of Proverbs 16:5 tells us the Lord hates the proud of heart. The second part of the verse goes on to say, "Be sure of this: They will not go unpunished."

The Bible offers many examples of God's wrath falling on the proud. In Daniel 4, for instance, Babylon's King Nebuchadnezzar walks on the roof of his palace and says, "Is this not the great Babylon I have built as the royal residence, by my mighty power and for the glory of my majesty?" (v. 30).

As human standards go, he had some reason to be proud. He had conquered all of the known world of his day and enslaved all its peoples. But God would not allow Nebuchadnezzar's pride to go unchecked. He was going to make an example for all time of that arrogant leader.

The words of verse 30 "were still on his lips when a voice came from heaven, 'This is what is decreed for you, King Nebuchadnezzar: Your royal authority has been taken from you. You will be driven away from people and will live with the wild animals; you will eat grass like cattle. Seven times [years] will pass by for you until you acknowledge that the Most High is sovereign over the kingdoms of men and gives them to anyone he wishes' " (vv. 31,32).

And that's exactly what happened.

Another time, King Herod of Israel gave a speech, and afterward the crowd said, "This is the voice of a god, not of a man."

"Immediately," we're told, "because Herod did not give praise to God, an angel of the Lord struck him down, and he was eaten by worms and died" (Acts 12:22,23).

Clearly, God takes a harsh view of pride, and it can lead to our destruction.

> *Humility is quiet about self.*

A somewhat humorous example of how pride can kill us comes from the ancient fable of the frog and the goose who became good friends. They sang duets together and helped each other find food. In general, they respected each other's gifts.

Then the fall of the year came, and it was time for the goose to fly south for the winter. The goose said he would like to take the frog with him, but he didn't know how they could do it. The frog suggested that he tie a string around the goose and then hold the other end with his mouth.

That's just what they did, and it worked fine as they flew high through the sky—until a farmer saw the strange sight and shouted out, "What a marvelous plan! Who thought of it?"

Bursting with pride, the frog could not resist shouting back, "I did!"

God's Way to Greatness

Pride is terribly destructive, but the opposite is also true: Humility isn't just good—it's God's way to greatness. First Peter 5:5,6 tells us, "Clothe yourselves with humility toward one another, because 'God opposes the proud but gives grace to the humble.' Humble yourselves, therefore, under God's mighty hand, that he may lift you up in due time." The New American Standard Bible translates that last part of the passage "that He may *exalt* you at the proper time" (my emphasis).

James 4:10 likewise reads, "Humble yourselves before the Lord, and he will lift you up" ("He will exalt you," NASB).

Jesus Himself told His disciples about how earthly rulers lord it over their subjects, and then He said, "Not so with you. Instead, whoever wants to become great among you must be your servant, and whoever wants to be first must be slave of all" (Mark 10:43,44). To drive home his point, He added, "For even the Son of Man did not come to be served, but to serve, and to give his life as a ransom for many" (v. 45).

Humility has power. Mankind's way to greatness is to focus on power, but God's way is to focus on submissiveness.

Man's way is to focus on freedom. God's way is to emphasize responsibility.

Man's way is concern for gain. God's way is concern for giving.

The world says greatness lies in having immediate fulfillment of our desires. God says it lies in the desire for lasting achievement, for eternal good.

Man says we should yearn for the praise of others. God says we should yearn for His approval.

The world says we become great when we push ahead while longing for self-gratification. God says we become great when we learn patience and self-control.

The world says we become great through competition. God says greatness is achieved through cooperation.

Finally, the world says we become great when we strive to be leaders of men, but God says we become great as we strive to follow Him.

The contrast couldn't be clearer between the pride of the world and the humility of God. The results of the two approaches are quite different.

There's not a power on earth that can stand up to God's kind of humility and submissiveness. It's impossible to threaten people who are hanging on a cross. What can you threaten them with? Oh, that we would nail our pride to that cross! Loving hearts do it every day.

Chapter Reflection

Humility is something you will soon get if you don't have it! Remember the story about the lady who was eating the man's cookies by mistake? Do you recall an incident that taught you humility?

Discussion Questions

1. What is humility? List some basic ingredients of humility?
2. Read Proverbs 21:4, Proverbs 8:13, Proverbs 16:5, 1 John 2:16 and 2 Timothy 3:2. Why is pride sinful? Why is it so destructive to a Christian? Can you recall biblical examples of how God dealt with pride?
3. God uses servant leaders in His church, but servant leadership is a difficult concept for most leaders. Who is our example of a servant leader? Why do you think God made servant leadership the pattern for the church?
4. The author quotes James 4:10: "Humble yourselves before the Lord, and He will lift you up." Do you believe this statement? How does it affect your life?

6

Encouraging Others

A pat on the back, though only a few vertebrae removed from a kick in the pants, is miles ahead in results.
(Royal Neighbor)

Shortly after the Civil War, in a New England mental institution, lived a small, partially blind girl known as Little Annie. She was kept locked in a basement room, considered hopelessly insane.

The only person who thought otherwise was an elderly nurse who each day would go down the stairs and eat her lunch near Annie. She refused to give up on the girl and kept encouraging her. She would leave brownies for her, which were ignored.

After awhile, though, Annie started eating the brownies. Then, gradually, ever so slowly, the little girl opened up to the nurse. Eventually, she got to the point where she could be put in with the other children, and she was found to be mentally sound. When she grew up, she didn't want to leave the institution. She wanted to stay and help other kids, so she became a teacher.

Now the story shifts to Great Britain a number of years later, where Queen Victoria was awarding England's highest civilian honor to Helen Keller. You may recall that Helen was a famous American author and lecturer who was blind and deaf and yet graduated with honors from Radcliffe College. The queen asked her, "How do you account for the fact that although you were both deaf and blind, you were able to accomplish so much?"

Without hesitation, Helen answered, "If it had not been for Annie Sullivan, the world would never have known of Helen Keller."

Annie Sullivan (later Anne Sullivan Macy), of course, was Little Annie. And not only was she the teacher who gave life and hope to Helen Keller, but she also pioneered techniques of education for the handicapped and helped promote the American Foundation for the Blind. Hers was a full, productive life of helping others.

Behind Helen Keller's great success, then, was Annie Sullivan. And behind Annie's success was the loving heart of an encouraging nurse whose name is forgotten to history but whose love lives on.

We read in 1 Corinthians 13:5, "[Love] is not self-seeking." It does not seek advantage or comfort for itself. It does not promote itself. It does not seek to get ahead by tearing others down. Instead, a loving heart seeks the good of others by encouraging them, believing in them, cheering them on to be and to do the best they can.

Everybody Needs It

A study was conducted at Springfield College in Massachusetts to see what effect the lack of encouragement had on children. A group of them were put in a room, and they were asked to draw a detailed picture of a man. When they finished, they were asked to draw another picture of a man, making this one better than the first. After they finished the second picture, they were told to draw a third, making it the best yet.

No matter how poor their drawings might have been, the kids were not criticized for their work. However, neither were they praised or given any encouragement. They were merely told to draw each of the three pictures.

You can probably guess the results. Some of the children showed resentment. One refused to do all three drawings. Most just got angry, said nothing, and continued the joyless, unrewarding toil. Each of their pictures, however, got progressively worse.

In another experiment that was reported in *Psychology Today*, college students were asked to report to the psychology professor's office one at a time to take a test. When a student arrived, the professor would say, "Come in and sit down, please. I'm going to read you a set of instructions, and I'm not permitted to say anything that's not in the instructions. Nor can I answer any questions about this exam. OK?"

The student was then given the test. After he finished, he would leave, and another student would arrive. The professor would repeat the instructions with the same exact words, but this time he would *smile* as he said them. That was the only difference in how the test was presented. Would the smile have any effect on how the students did with the test? That's what the experiment was designed to discover.

Once again, you've probably guessed the outcome. Just a simple smile, that little bit of encouragement, made a striking difference in how well the students performed. Those who received it did much better on the test.

Experiments like those only confirm what we all understand intuitively. Everybody needs encouragement. We all feel better and do better when we receive it. We all suffer without it.

One time I was planning to speak in Fresno, Calif., during the time of year (I think it was January) when fog can be a real problem there, especially at the airport. I had been fogged in the last time I visited Fresno. I was explaining this to my daughter, adding that I needed to get out of Fresno Saturday night so I could be back in my home church to preach Sunday morning.

"Well, we'll just pray about that," Elizabeth said.

Somehow that really struck me and stayed with me the whole trip. All the time I was in Fresno, whenever I thought about the fog and whether I'd be able to get out on schedule, I remembered that Elizabeth was praying for me, and I was tremendously encouraged. The fog did appear, as feared, but it opened up just in time for our plane to take off.

On the same trip, my host took me to a restaurant called the Iron Horse. I've never seen anything like it. When we went in, the waitresses greeted us and lead us to our table with a "Woo, woo, woo!" like a train whistle. Everybody was clapping and carrying on like you can't imagine.

After a minute one of the waitresses stopped everyone and said, "Hold it, hold it, everybody. We've got one from Texas here." They had me stand up and take a bow while the whole place applauded.

While we ate, my friend said, "We come here on Sundays, and you have to line up outside the door to get in." Why was that? Because the food was so great? No, the food was OK, but people stand in line to get in because the staff builds them up and makes them feel important. They gladly pay their money because they're so appreciated there.

> *"I always teach better when you are in my class."*

At another seminar, a man came up to me and said, "I heard you speak before, and you talked about forgiveness and restoring relationships." Then he told me about an old conflict he had had with his sister and how long it had been since they had talked to each other. He finished by saying, "I want you to know those things you said have changed my life. I went home and called my sister, and now we're talking to each other again."

That story is not told to pat myself on the back but to tell you how much encouragement I received from that man. I get discouraged, too. I travel and speak a lot, but sometimes I think, "I'm not very good at this. Other speakers are so much better! Am I helping anyone?"

Maybe you can understand a little of how that man's words made me feel. I was fantastically encouraged!

One man's memory of his favorite Sunday school teacher was that she came to visit him on Monday if he'd been sick the day before. She gave him a little five-cent trinket that was worth a million dollars to him. Then she said something like this: "Johnny, I always teach better when you're in my class. When you come next Sunday morning, would you raise your hand so I can see you're in attendance? Then I'll teach better."

The man said he noticed that from time to time, a lot of kids were raising their hands, and the class just got bigger and bigger.

Encouragement. We all need it, and we all respond to it.

Making It a Habit

Without even realizing it most of the time, we're either encouraging others or discouraging them all of the time. In every contact, we have either a positive or a negative impact, however small. And loving hearts, once they're aware of this, will make a habit of looking for ways to lift the spirits of every person they meet.

A poem by Edgar Guest captures this idea pretty well:

> I watched them tearing a building down,
> A gang of men in a busy town.
> With a ho-heave-ho and a lusty yell,
> They swung a beam, and the side wall fell.
> I asked a foreman: "Are these men skilled,
> As the men you'd hire if you had to build?"
> He gave a laugh and said: "No indeed!
> Just common labor is all you need.
> I can easily wreck in a day or two
> What builders have taken a year to do."
>
> And I thought to myself as I went my way,
> Which of the roles have I tried to play?
> Am I a builder who works with care,
> Measuring life by the rule and square?

> Am I shaping my deeds to a well-made plan,
> Patiently doing the best I can?
> Or am I a wrecker who walks the town,
> Content with the labor of tearing down?

We're builders or we're wreckers; we're balcony people, pulling others up, or we're basement people, pulling them down. Let's make it our habit to be builders and balcony people. In Hebrews 10:24,25, we're commanded to do just that: "And let us consider how we may spur one another on toward love and good deeds. Let us not give up meeting together, as some are in the habit of doing, but let us encourage one another—and all the more as you see the Day approaching."

One warning, though—that fatigue is one of our greatest enemies in developing such a habit. When we get tired, we have a hard time thinking clearly and acting right. So take special care when you're tired not to let slip a careless word or deed.

I remember one time when Bobbie and I experienced the humorous side of how fatigue affects us. We had both had a difficult day, and we were getting ready to go out to dinner. I puffed and let out a big sigh to show how tired I was, and Bobbie said, "Oh, I need to be petting my baby, but I'm too pooped to pet." Vince Lombardi put it this way: "Fatigue makes cowards of us all."

Good News

If you'll work at making it a habit to encourage others, you'll discover that it's the very best way to live. There's nothing like it if you want to stay young, energetic, enthusiastic and filled with life and joy. If you want to cheer up, cheer up someone else.

A man named Travis Rusheon Dardell wrote about an incident when he proved the truth of this principle. He was stuck at a traffic light one day, and he glanced out of his car window into a music shop, where a piano was on display. A man sat at the keyboard, playing for all he was worth.

"Though I could not hear a single note," Dardell wrote, "I watched him play his song. And when he had finished, he caught my eye. I held my hands up and applauded rapidly and silently mouthed the words, 'Bravo, bravo.' He stood and turned in my direction, and there in the store window, bowed deeply in his best maestro fashion. Then we both laughed. The light changed, and I drove off, pleased with myself, my fellow man and life in general."

Thomas Malone once observed that most emotional problems can be summed up as a person walking around screaming, "For God's sake, love me!" On the other hand, he said, healthy people are those walking around looking for someone to love. And if you see positive changes in the people with the problems, it's because they've realized that if they give up the screaming and start loving another person, they'll finally get the love they've been screaming for all their lives. "It's hard to learn," Malone said, "but it's good when you learn it."

> *We can't do better for ourselves than to help others.*

We can't do better for ourselves than to help others. Earl Nightingale told a story about a 6-year-old girl and her brother, who had been stricken with infantile paralysis. They lived near a railroad track where the streamliner City of Denver went speeding by once a week.

One day, the little girl was seen pulling her helpless brother in a wagon up to the fence beside the track. She scanned the rails for the train, which she knew should be coming soon. And when she heard its whistle in the distance, she flew into action. She pulled her heavy brother out of the wagon, raised him to a standing position so he could grasp the top rail of the fence, then lowered her head and pressed it into his back to hold him steadily erect as the train flashed by.

Afterward, an amazed onlooker exclaimed with concern, "Darling, you didn't get to see the train at all yourself!"

Encouraging Others 65

The little girl paused at her task of getting her brother back in the wagon and said softly, "I saw it before he got sick." Putting others ahead of ourselves is the way we save ourselves.

Bad News

If the good news is that we help ourselves by encouraging others and putting them first, the bad news is that the opposite is also true. Selfishness and neglecting to encourage hurts others, and it also hurts us.

In Matthew 18:15, Jesus told us, "If your brother sins against you, go and show him his fault, just between the two of you." In my opinion, that's the most violated passage in the Bible. Don't talk to your brother's coach or his spouse or the neighbors or your friends at church. Go talk directly to the person involved.

I recall a chapel speaker who, in encouraging others to give to a certain program, stated that he had given and hoped others would also.

Afterward, he was critized in the editorial of the school paper. "Such display as this makes one ask, 'Where are the trumpets?' "

How that must have hurt the speaker! And the writer probably never considered his violation of Scripture. If he had gone to the spaker, he would have learned of his sincerity in raising funds. He could then have been an encourager.

Where is the license to publicly rebuke a fellow Christian instead of going to him privately? It happens all over the brotherhood, hurting feelings and relationships and bringing disrepute on the cause of Christ. We need to be very careful what we say and what we write.

The Bible is full of examples of people who sought not to encourage and serve others but to advance their own selfish interests—and who were destroyed in the process. Think of Lot, choosing the best land for himself near Sodom and Gommorah. Think of Achan, hiding stolen riches from Jericho and bringing judgment on himself and his whole family. Think of

Nabal, refusing to share his abundance with David's men and being stricken dead as a result. Think of Ananias and Sapphira, who lied about what they were giving to the church and ended in tragedy.

If love is not self-seeking, it should come as no surprise that unloving selfishness can only hurt us. He who is full of himself is very empty indeed.

How We Can Encourage Others

How do we go about encouraging others? It doesn't take some big, special effort. We can do it in a thousand little ways every day. Let me offer just a few suggestions.

First, a simple smile can do wonders. I described the college experiment earlier showing how just a smile caused students to do better on a test. A smile in such a situation conveys a feeling of confidence, an expectation that the person is going to do well, which somehow we human beings try to live up to. It also releases the tension in the air.

> *People put forth greater effort under a spirit of approval.*

How do we look to our children? Do we smile at them often? It's so simple, but it can make a big difference. Studies have shown that the parents of delinquent kids are habitually *nonsmiling* people. By their grimness, they convey a message to their children that says, "You're not really loved; you're not really wanted; you're not really accepted."

Second, a kind word can do wonders. Words of approval, words of praise, words of encouragement can make a world of difference. Charles Schwab, a great salesman and industrialist around the turn of the century, once said, "In my wide association in life, meeting many great men in various parts of the world, I have yet to find the man, however great or exalted his station, who did not do better work and put forth greater effort under a spirit of approval than he would ever do under a spirit of criticism."

I have great attendance and punctuality in my college classes, even in the 7:40 a.m. class. Some teachers find it difficult to believe that students are in class so early in the morning. You know how I do it? I just thank those who come on time. That's all. Nothing is said about those who are tardy—I just keep thanking those who are punctual. And most of them make it on time. There has to be some correlation here!

The tone of voice we use also can make a great difference. A refugee had finally found a job here in America after several months, but hadn't yet been able to save enough money to send for his wife. One day he received a letter from her, written in English by a helpful person in the refugee camp where she lived. Since he couldn't read English, he asked a neighbor to read it to him.

The neighbor was an ill-tempered, mad-at-the-world type with a grumpy voice. So he read in an angry tone, "Why haven't you sent for me? I need the money right away."

The immigrant grabbed the letter from his neighbor's hand and said, "She has no right to speak to me like that! I'm doing the best I can!"

A few weeks later, he received another letter from his wife, again in English. This time he asked a gentle, compassionate, young man to read it to him. In a soft, pleasant voice, the young man read, "Did you get my last letter? Why haven't you sent for me? I need the money right away."

"Well," said the immigrant, "that's better. If she hadn't changed her tone, I wouldn't have sent for her."

The tone of voice we use is so important. Think of how babies respond to tone of voice. They don't understand any of the words we say to them, but they clearly pick up how we feel toward them by *how* we speak. It's really no different as adults. The way something is said is as important as—maybe even more important than—the words that are used.

Third, we encourage by acts of love and kindness. Dr. Richard Selzer, in his book *Mortal Lessons*, tells the story of a young patient from whose cheek he had to remove a tumor. Unfortunately, in doing that, a small nerve had been severed, and the young woman's face was now twisted in a clownish, permanent way.

When her husband first came into her room after the operation, he stood next to her bed, and they touched each other tenderly. The woman asked Dr. Selzer, "Will my mouth always be like this?"

"Yes, it will," he answered, "because the nerve is cut."

She nodded in somber silence.

But her husband smiled and said, "I like it. It's kind of cute." And then he bent over his wife to kiss her, twisting his own lips to fit hers and show her they could still kiss. What love! What encouragement wrapped up in a simple act that was exactly what she needed!

Fourth, we can encourage others just by being good listeners. Most of us like to hear ourselves talk, but there are a lot of hurting people out there who need someone to listen. Often, that's the best way we can show we care.

A young man wrote a letter to Ann Landers in which he really covered all the points I've tried to convey in this section. One of his friends had committed suicide, and the young man himself had tried to do the same. he wrote,

> *If people want to help, they can. Here are a few things anybody can do. Smile more even to people you don't know. Touch people. Look them in the eye. Let them know you're aware they exist. Be concerned about those you work with. Listen when they talk to you. Spend an extra minute. If someone has a problem, just listening means more than you'll ever know.*

As already stated, encouraging others and putting them first doesn't take a lot of effort or require grandiose gestures. But we do have to stop and think about what we say and do. We do have to get in the habit of looking for opportunities to build others up. And when we do, we'll be richly rewarded in ways we can't even imagine.

Jesus told His disciples that they needed to be like children in their faith (Matthew 18:3-5), and a beautiful story that makes a fitting way to end this chapter comes from a group of people who embody a lot of what He was talking about.

The event was the 440-yard race in the Special Olympics, which is where special people compete. This little guy was way out in front of the pack as they headed down the home stretch, so far ahead that he turned to look back and see where the rest of the runners were. But in doing that, he stumbled and fell.

Before he could get up and take off again, the rest of the kids caught up with him. They could have run right by him and beat him to the tape. But do you know what they did? They all stopped and picked him up, and then everyone ran on to the finish line together.

There were no losers in that race. They were all winners. And if we could pick up just a little of the love that filled their hearts, we would all be winners, too.

Chapter Reflection

Encouragement is consistently appreciated. What is it about an "encourager" that is always welcome?

Discussion Question

1. Research indicates a human need for encouragement. Do you believe that is true? Explain.

2. If it is true that we help ourselves by encouraging others and by putting them first, do you agree that selfishness hurts others and also hurts us? Explain.

3. If it is in our own self interest to act positive for others and to encourage others, then why don't we see more encouragement practiced?

4. Read 1 Thessalonians 5:11-14 and Hebrews 3:13. What do these passages say about encouragement? What are some practical ways we can encourage others?

7

Keeping a Long Fuse

*Folks who fly into a rage
always make a bad landing.
(Globe Gazette)*

A man we'll call John, who had been in one of my seminars, wrote to tell me of an interesting change in his habits. He explained that in the past, every day, on his way home from work, he fought the traffic all the way. He rushed to get home as soon as he could. Red lights, slow drivers and other drivers cutting in front of him drove him nuts.

By the time he got home, John said, he was a nervous wreck. His stomach was tied in knots. He was frustrated, worn out and angry. He often found himself snapping at his wife and kids for no good reason. Needless to say, his evenings—not to mention his relationships with his family—left something to be desired. And it was all because he let the freeway traffic get to him so badly.

Finally, after several years of living that way, a light clicked on in John's mind. He realized how unproductive and even harmful his approach to the drive home was, and he determined that he would make some changes. He would simply drive more slowly, not pushing to finish the trip as quickly as possible. He would relax and not be so competitive when another driver went around or cut in front of him.

Here's what happened: The first time John tried this new approach, on the same road, at the same time of day, it took him *only two minutes longer* to get home. But the difference in his attitude was like the difference between night and day. Arriving at the house, he was calm, relaxed and ready to show love to his wife and children. His emotions were under control.

Notice that his situation hadn't changed. He was still stopped by red lights, cut off by rude drivers and sometimes stuck behind slowpokes. But once he decided to stay in control and not get angry, all he lost was two minutes. That was nothing compared to what he gained in return.

We read in 1 Corinthians 13:5, "[Love] is not provoked." In other words, love is not touchy. Loving hearts don't have short fuses. Like John, they've learned that patience isn't just a virtue—it's simply the best way to live. James 1:19, 20 puts it this way: "Everyone should be quick to listen, slow to speak and slow to become angry, for man's anger does not bring about the righteous life that God desires." Proverbs 29:11 tells us that the loving approach is also the way of wisdom: "A fool gives full vent to his anger, but a wise man keeps himself under control."

Why We Become Angry

What causes us to become angry, anyway? What accounts for our short fuses? We need to explore at least several reasons.

For one thing, we become angry when people show what we consider a lack of respect for us. We have an image of ourselves and how we should be treated, and when people don't give us that measure of honor, we become offended and angry.

This is the kind of indignation we would feel at a dinner party if we were seated at the far end of the table or if an important person there ignored us. It's seen in churches all the time when a prestigious job is given to one person and not another. The root problem, in other words, is ego or conceit. It's the opposite of the humility identified as a habit of loving hearts in chapter 5.

A second reason we become angry is that we think some right of ours has been violated. We tend to believe we're entitled to uninterrupted good health, growing prosperity and warm, wonderful relationships. We want to be happy all the time, never sad or frustrated. And when we're denied one of these "rights"—when we or our loved ones get sick, when we lose our jobs, when we have marital conflict or trouble with our kids—we become angry.

> *Christians have privileges rather than rights.*

The fact is, however, that we have no such rights. Here in America, we've been tremendously blessed and privileged, enjoying a lifestyle and a level of security and good health that are the envy of much of the rest of the world. But those things aren't *rights*. Members of the early church suffered in every way—even death by torture—because of their faith (Hebrews 11). That was totally consistent with what Jesus and His apostles told them to expect. For example, Peter wrote, "Dear friends, do not be surprised at the painful trial you are suffering, as though something strange were happening to you. But rejoice that you participate in the sufferings of Christ, so that you may be overjoyed when his glory is revealed" (1 Peter 4:12,13).

That's the perspective we *ought* to have, but of course it's much easier to read that than it is to do it. Still, the more we can realize that we have privileges rather than rights, the less we'll fly off the handle when our will is frustrated.

A third reason we become angry is that, unfortunately, we often get what we want by our anger. Other people may be intimidated into yielding to our desires. Some will give in just to avoid further conflict, and anger works for us.

What we forget, though, is the price we pay to win that way. Hurt feelings, loss of love, greater resistance, possible physical harm when we insist on our "rights" on the road, or damage to our witness for Christ—these are just some of the costs of winning through anger.

Three Things That Tell a Lot

Over the years, I've learned that you can tell a lot about people by observing three things concerning them: (1) How often do they become angry? People who have their emotions and desires under control—people with loving hearts—become angry a lot less often than others. They're more eventempered, they enjoy life more and others enjoy being around them more. Others also aren't afraid to talk to them because they don't have to worry that they'll fly into a rage whenever there's a difference of opinion.

(2) What things do they become angry about? People who have a problem with anger get upset over every little thing they don't like or anything that frustrates their plans. Have you ever been in a car with someone like this at the wheel—someone like the John at the beginning of the chapter? Every slow driver, everyone who blocks his ability to change lanes or make a turn when he wants and every red light is seen as an enemy. As his passenger, by the time you get to your destination, you've been reduced to a nervous wreck.

On the other hand, people in control of their emotions become angry only over important things. Usually, those are things threatening harm to others, not their own "rights." Their anger is reserved not for life's inevitable irritations, but for those people and situations that have the potential to hurt the innocent. In those cases, anger is the only appropriate response.

Dr. Carol Travis, in his book about anger, told a story about a swami in an Indian village who had mastered anger. When his ability of control over his anger was challenged, he told about a big, old cobra that used to bite people on their way to worship at the temple. The swami went to visit with the snake and to bring it under submission. He told the snake it was wrong to bite people, and he persuaded the serpent never to do it again.

When the people saw that the snake no longer made any move to bite them, they grew unafraid. Before long, the village boys were dragging the poor cobra behind them while they ran laughing here and there.

The swami again visited the snake to see if it was keeping its promise not to bite humans. The cobra humbly and miserably approached the man. "You're bleeding!" the swami said. "Tell me how this has come to be."

The snake, near tears, blurted out that he'd been abused ever since he was forced to make his promise.

Shaking his head, the swami said, "I told you not to bite, but I didn't say you couldn't hiss."

In the face of evil, when people are threatening or actually abusing us or others, it's OK to hiss.

Even Jesus became angry. You'll recall that one time, when He entered Jerusalem and went to the temple, He became angry enough to drive out those who were buying and selling there and to overturn the tables of the money changers and the benches of those selling doves for sacrifice. Why? Not because of the kinds of slights or irritations that anger us but because His Father's name was being dishonored.

"Is it not written: 'My house will be called a house of prayer for all nations'? But you have made it 'a den of robbers' " (Mark 11:15-17).

The things that anger people tell us a lot about them.

Finally, we learn a lot from how long people stay angry once they become so. Most of us, once we become angry, find it difficult to get ourselves back under control. "Starting a quarrel is like breaching a dam," we read in Proverbs 17:14. Once we get that flow started, we've got a flood on our hands.

I've certainly experienced that in my own life. I remember times when I was tempted to become angry with Bobbie but was able instead to stay cool and calm. We were able to communicate, and it was beautiful. I also remember, with horror, some times when I wasn't successful in doing that and as a result will forever regret things said in anger. We simply can't say everything we think and build relationships!

Here's more wisdom from Proverbs: "The heart of the righteous weighs its answers" (15:28). Wise and righteous people think *carefully* about what they're going to say and how others will receive it and be affected by it before they say it. "But," the verse goes on to say, "the mouth of the wicked gushes evil."

That sounds like me when I became angry and a volcano erupted. I didn't even realize at the moment what I was saying. Anger begets anger. It's like blowing hot air into a balloon—the more you blow, the tighter the balloon gets, and the more it wants to explode.

Loving hearts, however, are not only slow to become angry, but they're also quick to let go of it. They don't hold grudges. They don't plot how to get even with someone who slighted them. They don't make mountains of resentment out of life's frustrations. They get on with the business and joy of living, forgiving when they need to forgive and making the most of their blessings. They've learned to apply the wisdom of Ephesians 4:26, 27: " 'In your anger do not sin': Do not let the sun go down while you are still angry, and do not give the devil a foothold."

Paul is saying there that if we take anger, embellish it, draw it to our bosom, make it a friend and let it stay with us for periods of time—if we do that, we just open the door for the devil to march in with all his evil and wickedness. That's why Paul urges us near the end of that chapter, "Get rid of all bitterness, rage and anger, brawling and slander, along with every form of Malice" (4:31). If we don't, we open ourselves and those we love to a world of hurt.

How Anger Hurts Us

Not only does uncontrolled anger hurt us and others; anger is also devastating because it emotionally *blocks our logic*. We get caught up in it and keep spewing and venting it without realizing that we're doing tremendous damage. We don't know enough to stop, and sometimes, when we lose control, we can't even stop when we want to.

One father told me of incidents he can remember which always wrack him with guilt, times when he became so angry with his young son that he shouted things he didn't really mean but couldn't stop saying, even as his boy cried his heart out. That father, who really does love his son deeply, just became consumed by his anger so that it was controlling him instead of the other way around. He would give anything to be able to go back and live those times over in a better way, but that's impossible. Once the hurtful words have been said, we can never take them back or change them.

Unfortunately, I can relate all too well to that father's experience. As a father and as a coach, I turned red-faced and embarrassed when I think back on the past. My close friends could probably relate some things I said and did, but fortunately they are gracious people and kind enough not to remind me often.

> *What angers us controls us.*

The reference to my friends leads to another way anger hurts us: It lessens the respect people have for us. Maybe our friends and loved ones will forgive and forget an occasional fit of anger, recognizing we're human. But if we become angry habitually—if it's our standard way of getting what we want or if we're just out of control—others will lose some repsect for us every time it happens. And some who see our outbursts, such as co-workers, neighbors or people at the store or church, won't be tolerant and understanding at all.

Think of a time when you saw someone, perhaps a parent, who lost control in a public display of anger. How did you react? What did you think of that person? If the person was a stranger, would you have been inclined to invite him or her to your home for coffee? If it was someone you knew, how was your perception of the person changed?

However you reacted to that person, that's the way others

are thinking of you when you lose your temper in public. There's no quicker way to lose the respect of others.

People who are frequently angry are also apt to be sick a lot. Continued inappropriate anger takes a heavy toll on body, mind and spirit. It heightens the heart rate, breathing rate and other bodily functions, preparing a person to fight. When the body stays in that state over long periods, it just wears out. And a tired body is one that's more susceptible to disease of all kinds.

Anger also wears us out mentally and emotionally. We become preoccupied with it so that we can't think straight or concentrate on other things. We can't enjoy the good things in life—we don't even recognize we have them. We can push others away, even when they want to love us and support us. Anger is a relationship killer, plain and simple.

Spiritually, wrongful anger is a sin, so it cuts us off from fellowship with God. When we nurse it, we're not forgiving as we should. We're not giving thanks to God as we should. We're certainly not giving an attractive witness of God's love. And in that condition, our spiritual batteries will quickly run down to the point where the meter showing our inner vitality can barely flicker.

In short, an easily aroused temper destroys us in every phase of life. Angry people are headaches to themselves and heartaches to everyone else. Letting ourselves be controlled by anger simply is not being smart. It's stupid, and it's a sin against God.

Controlling Our Anger

How, then, do we get control of our anger and avoid all that pain? Let me offer some battle-tested suggestions.

First, we have to admit we anger easily. Denying the problem will only prolong the pain. Besides, when we deny our tendency to lose our temper, we're only fooling ourselves. To everyone else, our short fuse is all too obvious.

Second, when we feel ourselves becoming angry, we need to just *stop*. Just pull ourselves up short when we see it coming on, before we lose control. We've all heard about counting to 10 before we speak. Some of us may need to count to 100 or even 1,000! But however high we need to count, *we need to get our emotions under control before we say one word.*

As a wise person once said, the easiest way to save face is to keep the lower half of it shut. A Chinese proverb says, "If you're patient in one moment of anger, you'll save a hundred days of sorrow." Or as another insightful person said, "Speak when you're angry, and you'll make the best (or maybe it's the worst) speech you'll ever regret."

Third, we can force ourselves to smile. It's almost impossible to be angry and smile at the same time. It's a simple, mechanical kind of thing to do, and if you're looking at other people when you do it, they might think you're diabolical. But it really works. You might even find yourself laughing as you think about what you look like!

A fourth approach is to just change what you're doing at the moment. Get away from whatever it is that's raising your ire. You can always come back to it later, when you've calmed down and reined in your emotions again. It's better to wait, even in disciplining disobedient children, than it is to speak or act in anger. Force yourself to walk away until you're under control and can do what's best in the situation rather than just venting your temper.

A fifth way is to mentally stand away from ourselves and look as objectively as we can at what's happening. The idea is to think back and write down the times when we've become angry recently. What upset us? What basic rights of ours did we feel were violated? Who else was involved? As we do this, we'll probably begin to see some patterns, some people and situations that "get us going" most every time.

Armed with that information, we'll be better prepared to deal with those situations the next time we encounter them. Maybe we can avoid some of them with a little planning. Maybe we need to talk to some folks about the way we relate together. Maybe we need to be praying more. Whatever the need, God can show us, perhaps with the help of others who know us and whom we can trust. Forwarned is forearmed!

A sixth key to controlling our anger is to change our belief system. We get mad, in part, because we think it benefits us. Otherwise, we wouldn't do it.

Three girls in my class were rooming together one term, and two of them told me about the other's bad temper. "We just stay out of her way," they said.

The other girl asked me, "Why do I have such a bad temper, anyway?"

"It's because you believe it's to your advantage to get mad," I said. "People get out of your way. But if you realized your anger isn't getting you what you really want, that it's alienating your friends, you'd just quit. You *can* control your anger—you already do. You only get angry to a certain degree—just enough to get them out of your way."

The truth is that while we usually think circumstances and people and situations upset us, we actually upset ourselves with our belief system. We're kind of like the lion tamer who put this ad in a show-business paper: "Lion tamer wants tamer lions." We'd like to have tamer situations and people to deal with, but that's not the answer. Changing the way we think is.

A seventh way to overcome anger is to take it one day at a time. That's really crucial to tackling any bad habit. If we stop anger one day at a time, at this present moment, we've controlled it. That's why Paul told us in Ephesians 4 not to let the sun go down on our anger. If we make it a practice not to go to bed angry but to do what's necessary to gain control of our emotions and mend relationships before the day is done, we'll be a lot further ahead. We'll be developing loving hearts.

Proverbs has the last word on this subject: "A gentle answer turns away wrath"—it dispels all the hot air—"but a harsh word stirs up anger" (15:1). Let's give the greatest gift we can to our families, to our spouses and children, as well as to our co-workers, neighbors and fellow church members. Let's stay cool, don't be easily ruffled, and get a long fuse. Let's learn to control our anger rather than letting it control us.

Chapter Reflections

It was once said that if you speak when you are angry, you will make the best speech you will ever wish you hadn't! Explain the passage in James 1:20: "For man's anger does not bring about the righteous life that God desires.

Discussion Questions

1. What are some of the reaons we become angry? Which of these is your particular challenge? Are any of these reasons justifable?
2. Can anger be used for good? Is it always bad or hurtful?
3. Can a person avoid ever becoming angry? What does a person's anger tell us about that person?
4. What does James 1:19 admonish us to do? Why do you think James mentioned "hearing" and "speaking" in relation to anger?
5. What are the seven steps the author suggests to control anger?

8

Holds No Grudges

*Forgiveness is the fragrance
the violet sheds on the heel
that has crushed it.*
     (Mark Twain)

A recent book called *It's Hard to Forgive* tells the story of a young woman who, while in college, in the bright years of her life, was abducted by a man, raped and murdered. Her killer was apprehended, convicted and sentenced to prison.

The girl's parents, rather than hating the man, started reaching out to him with letters offering love and forgiveness, attempting to teach him the truth of Christ's way. After trying for some time, they were finally granted an interview with him in prison, and they went to see him face to face.

According to the book, the mother said that when they saw the man who had killed their daughter, they hugged him and cried and told him they had forgiven him. As amazing as that is, there's more to the story.

Later, after the killer had committed his life to Christ, the girl's mother started traveling across the country, speaking about the joy and power of forgiveness, telling their story. How do you suppose her audiences responded? Were they overwhelmed with the faith and love of those parents? Did they rejoice over the salvation of a sin-darkened soul?

No, when the audiences heard about those parents' attitude toward the man who had killed their daughter, they actually grew hostile toward the woman! How could they possibly forgive the man who had done such horrible things to their daughter? It was inexcusable, the people said—beyond comprehension. Rather than forgiving him, the parents should have pushed for the full punishment of the law.

It is, indeed, difficult to forgive for a lot of reasons. Yet, that's exactly what we're called to do over and over in the Bible, and it's what loving hearts *do*. First Corinthians 13:5 tells us, "[Love] keeps no record of wrongs." In other words, a loving heart doesn't hold grudges. It doesn't keep a list of things people have said or done. In fact, the shorter the list of grievances we carry against others, the more love we have.

You can tell a lot about how loving people are by the things they remember and talk about. Some people have been badly hurt by others, and they spend the rest of their lives talking about it. Thirty, 40, even 50 years later, it's obvious they still carry grudges toward the ones they believe wronged them. Others who have been hurt just as badly talk instead about the good they've enjoyed and the positive things that are happening in their lives now. Theirs are the loving hearts.

In each book I've written, I have devoted an entire chapter to forgiveness and how important it is. So why should it be mentioned again in this book? Simply because we cannot talk about the habits of a *loving* heart and not include it. It's probably the most crucial habit of a loving heart. If in any way we discuss how to get along with each other or how to get the most out of life (which I usually do), we have to talk about *forgiveness*. It's central to every message.

The Urge for Revenge

As we saw by the response of people to a forgiving mother, we human beings have a natural and powerful urge for revenge. Partly, it's an outgrowth of our desire to see justice done, but that good intention often gets wrapped up in meanness and bitterness as well. In his book *Who Speaks for*

God?, Charles Colson says a new game is on the market called Capital Punishment. It's kind of like Monopoly, except that you don't buy houses and collect $200 when you pass Go. Instead, players each have four criminals they're responsible to punish. The object of the game is to get your criminals past the liberals and into the electric chair before your opponents do. The first contestant to execute all four of his or her criminals is the winner.

The manufacturer advertises the game as a way to "allow citizens frustrated by violent crimes to punish criminals vicariously." Sales of the game were reported to be brisk in hundreds of retail stores.

Our clinging to a desire for revenge and unwillingness to forgive hurts *us* more than anyone else. Jesus commanded us to love those who hurt us: "But I tell you: Love your enemies and pray for those who persecute you, that you may be sons of your Father in heaven" (Matthew 5:44,45). And He told us that as much for *our* good as for the good of those who need our forgiveness.

When the poet Edwin Markham reached the age of retirement, he discovered that his banker had defrauded him. Instead of being set for life, Markham was penniless. He was also bitter, obsessed with the evil done to him by a man he had thought was his friend.

Markham was so bitter, in fact, that he could no longer write poetry. His thoughts and emotions were too caught up in his pain and resentment.

And then one day, as he sat at his desk doodling and thinking about the man who had wronged him (*not* writing poetry), a thought came to him: "Markham, if you do not deal with this thing, it's going to ruin you. You cannot afford the price you are paying. You must forgive the man."

And then he wrote this poem, perhaps his most famous:

> He drew a circle that shut me out—
> Heretic, rebel, a thing to flout.
> But love and I had a wit to win:
> We drew a circle that took him in.

Forgiving the man proved to be Markham's deliverance, both personally and in his writing. We, too, need to forgive for our own peace of mind and heart, not to mention our physical health. Holding on to a grudge, like harboring inappropriate anger (the two are closely connected), can weaken our bodies and cause ulcers or leave us open to other illnesses.

It seems to me that more lives are spoiled by bitterness and lack of forgiveness than anything else. And the longer we carry a grudge, the heavier it becomes. We just can't afford to do it. It costs too much!

Two children, a brother and sister, were born to a father who was a slave to alcohol. All their lives, they remembered how he, in their early years, abused them and hurt them time after time. Both of them experienced the same pain and had the same reasons to be bitter, yet their lives turned out very differently.

The sister never forgave her father. She was bitter and miserable and full of hate right up until the day she died. She never got past those childhood emotional scars, and it cost her all the love and joy she could have experienced.

The brother, on the other hand, was amazingly sweet. He enjoyed a peace his sister never knew. How did he manage to find so much more joy in life when he came out of the same painful background?

Not long ago, the answer came clear to me when I saw the brother at his father's grave, placing flowers. His eyes were full of tears, and he said, "Dad, once again, I do forgive you for the way you made us suffer through the years." As hard as those words were to say, he meant them, and they had made a night-and-day difference between him and his bitter sister.

Think of Joseph, sold into Egyptian slavery by his brothers and then wrongly imprisoned (Genesis 37-50). He had every reason to be a very bitter man, to harbor hatred toward his jealous brothers. But he forgave them, and he had a healthy perspective on all that occurred: "Don't be afraid," he told them. "Am I in the place of God? You intended to harm me, but God intended it for good to accomplish what is now being done, the saving of many lives" (Genesis 50:19,20). Bitterness on Joseph's part could have cost many lives, but instead he enjoyed the privilege of rescuing them and having a family reunion to boot!

Obstacles to Forgiveness

Why is it so difficult to forgive?

For one thing, the non-Christian world sees forgiveness very differently and as a result doesn't support the Christian desire to forgive. The world says we're weaklings and cowards if we forgive too easily or too quickly. It's easy to get caught up in that mentality but difficult to go against it.

Ann Landers received a letter from a lawyer saying that years before, he had thrown a pie in the face of a teacher. Now he was regretting that, feeling guilty, and wondering how he could make up for it. Could he perhaps send $25 to pay for having the teacher's dress cleaned?

Well, Ann received a ton of mail in response to his letter, and the great majority of the letters said the teacher should *never* forgive him. Even though it was years before, and regardless of what he might do to make amends, the people thought he should never be forgiven.

That's the kind of sentiment that prevails in our world today, and it's difficult to swim against the tide.

Another obstacle to forgiveness is our pride. We want to teach the person who hurt us a lesson, and we're determined to do that to soothe our wounded egos, regardless of the cost.

A woman who was hospitalized with a severe ulcer and had suicidal tendencies had never forgiven her husband, who had engaged in an affair. Eventually, they were divorced and even though it had been several years since the affair (her former husband probably didn't even care about her opinion anymore), she still thought she was somehow punishing her husband by refusing to forgive. Her pride wouldn't let her admit that he had left her without caring. Neither would she admit that she was only hurting herself by failing to forgive him and get on with her life.

We have to want the peace that comes only with forgiveness enough that we *choose* to forgive. We have to recognize the benefits and decide that they outweigh the supposed benefits of seeking revenge. We have to give up on "teaching a lesson" to those who have wronged us.

> *Give up the right to get even.*

Forgiveness is also difficult because in order for it to happen and a relationship to be restored, someone has to make the first move, and neither party wants to do that. To do so, we think, is an admission that the other person was more right than we were—or, conversely, that we're more in the wrong.

Loving hearts, however, don't debate who goes first or who was more right. They simply seek to mend the relationship. There's a rule in sailing that says the more-maneuverable ship give right of way to the less-maneuverable ship. That's a good rule to follow in human relations, as well. Loving hearts take the initiative to make things right between people.

How to Forgive

Forgiving others starts with forgiving ourselves. When we realize how much we've been forgiven by God, we're able to forgive ourselves, and also those who harm us. Sometimes, though, that's difficult to do.

I received a heartbreaking letter from a middle-aged lady. She was a single lady who had been raped. After a few weeks, she discovered she had become pregnant as a result. She had severe medical problems—diabetes, high blood pressure and a heart condition. Combined with her age, those problems led her doctors to advise her to get an abortion.

Much to her sorrow, and with great resentment toward the doctors, she followed their counsel. She told me in her letter, "It was a very foolish thing I agreed to do when I agreed to have the abortion—a decision I'll regret for the rest of my life.

I'll never forgive myself." She added that she wanted to talk to me but that she was too ashamed, and she didn't sign her name, so I haven't been able to contact her.

You may not have done anything as drastic as that lady, but you may still be weighed down with guilt over something

> *Love never debates who goes first.*

you've said or done. To you and to her I would say, you probably *can't* forgive yourself *by yourself*. But I think *you can accept God's forgiveness*. And if you can, in time you'll be able to forgive yourself.

We all want and need forgiveness. I like the way Ruth Graham, wife of Billy Graham, said it. She and Billy were driving their car, and they passed through several construction areas where they had to slow down and go on a single-lane detour. Then, finally, they came to the end of the construction, and Ruth saw a sign that caught her attention.

"There," she said, pointing to the sign, "that's what I want on my tombstone."

Billy didn't get it at first, but then her meaning began to dawn on him, and he smiled.

The sign said, "End of construction. Thanks for your patience." That's another way of saying, in personal terms, "Thanks for extending me love. Thanks for forgiving me."

Another way to enjoy the blessings of forgiveness is to make a practice of going to bed each night with the feeling that you don't have an enemy in the world. Begin by sitting for half an hour each night and mentally forgiving all the people against whom you have any ill will, sending them thoughts of love. And if you've accused anyone unjustly or discussed anyone unkindly, if you have criticized or gossiped, withdraw your words by asking the Lord in silence to forgive you. If you've had a falling out with relatives or friends or there's a bone of contention between you and someone else, resolve to do all you can tomorrow to end the separation. Pray for your adversaries. Then you'll be ready for bed.

A Life-Changing Experience

Forgiving others is not only as much for our benefit as it is for others'. It is, in fact, a life-changing experience of the healthy kind. This was clearly exhibited in a weekend seminar of college-age students. We were covering the consequences of a lack of forgiveness and, among other areas, applied it to the relationship with their parents. In the session, one young man told the group that he just realized he never had forgiven his mom and dad for getting a divorce. He was especially bitter and angry toward his father.

> *Go to bed each day feeling that you don't have an enemy in the world.*

During the lunch break, rather than eating, he made a list of all the reasons he had for refusing to love and forgive his parents. Then he made a list of all the reasons he *should* love and forgive.

Next, he tore up the list of all the reasons not to forgive. "I felt so good when I did that!" he told the group.

Finally, he wrote a letter to each of his parents, telling them he had not forgiven them before but extending them forgiveness now, and he signed his name with love. He beamed as he told the group again, "I've never felt so good!"

The other young people applauded, got up and hugged him. It was a beautiful, life-changing experience for him. He then was ready to move on with his life.

We, too, can have life-changing experiences if we, like that young man, will follow the admonition of Colossians 3:12-14:

Therefore, as God's chosen people, holy and dearly loved, clothe yourselves with compassion, kindness, humility, gentleness and patience. Bear with each other and forgive whatever grievances you may have against one another. Forgive as the Lord forgave you. And over all these virtues put on love, which binds them all together in perfect unity.

Rudyard Kipling once said, "Nothing is ever settled until it is settled right." It's never settled right until it has been touched by the grace of forgiveness.

Chapter Reflection

Is it possible to go through life and not be wronged at some point by others? What are some reasons why people hurt one another?

Discussion Questions

1. Is a grudge a bad *feeling* toward another person for a wrong? Is it *doing* something harmful to the other person? Is it having sour *thoughts* about another person? What makes a grudge?
2. What does the author mean when he says we "cannot afford" to have a grudge?
3. Read Matthew 6:14,15, Matthew 18:35 and Mark 11:25. What is the principle in each of these passages? Give examples of how this principle should influence our actions.
4. How was it possible for Joseph not to bear a grudge against his brothers for what they did to him? How can we avoid holding grudges?
5. What are some obstacles to forgiveness? What are some selfish benefits of forgiveness?

9

Drawn to the Truth

The shortest and surest way to live with honor in the world is to be in reality what we appear to be.
(Socrates)

David Augsburger tells a story of three turtles who started out for a picnic. One carried the sandwiches, relish and dessert, while another carried the turtle-ade. The third wasn't carrying anything.

All of a sudden, they felt a few drops of rain. You can't have a picnic without an umbrella if it's raining, so they thought about who should go back to get the umbrella. They odd-turtled out, and the empty-legged one lost, so he was chosen.

"I won't go!" he said. "Just as soon as I leave, you're going to eat all the sandwiches and all the dessert, and there won't be anything left for me."

"No, we won't do that," the other two assured him. "We'll wait on you—no matter how long it takes."

"No matter how long it takes?"

"No matter. We'll wait."

"All right, then," he said, "I'll go."

So they sat there and waited for him. They waited an hour, two hours, all day, two days, a week, and finally two whole weeks. At last one of them said to the other, "You know, I think we might as well go ahead and eat."

Just then a little voice came from behind a bush saying, "If you do, I won't go!"

It's hard to trust people—even turtles. That's more true today than it's ever been before. In 1924, *Liberty* magazine sent a dollar to 100 people, and with it they included this message: "Here is your refund that you requested." None of those people had actually requested a refund—the editors wanted to see how many would be honest enough to admit that and return the money.

In 1924, they received 27 of those dollars back with notes saying there had been some mistake. In 1971, they did the test again, and that time they got back only 13 dollars. Today, they're afraid to run the test because they doubt they'd get anything back.

We find in 1 Corinthians 13:6, "Love does not delight in evil but rejoices with the truth." That means loving hearts are drawn to the truth. They're committed to honesty. They have integrity. They can be depended upon to do what they've promised to do.

Sadly, however, far too many people these days fail this test of a loving heart. An average, typical guy told his friend that a grocery store clerk had given him a phony dollar bill that morning. "You can't trust anybody," he said.

"Oh, let me look at it," the friend answered.

"Well, I've already passed it on at the drugstore," the first guy said.

That seems to be the way life goes today. You can't trust anybody. Something deadly is happening to American character in the halls of Congress, in corporate meeting rooms, in our cities and on our farms. We're fast becoming known as a nation of cheaters. We cheat in the classroom, on our taxes, on our spouses and on our employers.

Our Need to Trust

God made us to be trusting individuals. Our entire lives are built on trust. We can't exist without it. Every time we get in a car, we're trusting the engineers who designed it, the factory workers who built it and the mechanic who last serviced it. When we buy a box of cereal in the store, we're trusting that the farmer who grew the grain, the plant workers where the cereal was made and packaged, the truck driver and the store clerk have all handled it in a safe and sanitary way.

Bobbie and I spent some time in St. Louis once, and we went to the top of the Gateway Arch while we were there. To do that, you've got to have a lot of faith in the integrity and honesty of the people who built it.

Without doubt, trust is *essential* to marriage. If that trust is destroyed, the marriage explodes—marriage simply can't survive without it. That's why, whenever I speak to young people, I warn them not to marry just because someone they met makes their heart beat faster. Drinking too much coffee or cola will do that. You've got to have more than the tingles. I know love is blind, but it doesn't have to be stupid.

> *A pure heart is more important than a pretty face.*

A pure heart is more important than a pretty face. And young people looking for a life's partner need to check out the character of those they find romantically interesting. If anyone they are attracted to doesn't have integrity, they shouldn't just walk away from the relationship—they should run.

Just imagine what this world would be like if we couldn't trust anybody. You couldn't rely on the safety or performance of any of the products you buy, like the shampoo or toothpaste you use every morning. You couldn't trust your spouse to do anything to help you or to be faithful to you. You couldn't expect any of the other drivers on the highway to obey the traffic laws unless it was to their advantage. You couldn't depend on your employer to put anything into your retirement fund or even to pay you in full come payday. In short, life would be impossible.

We just can't live in dishonest relationships. Trust is the foundation on which they have to be built. Otherwise, we could never let ourselves be vulnerable, never open up and share our souls, never let our loved ones out of our sight.

Richard Freeman told a story that illustrates well the necessity of a stable foundation. A long time ago, before train engineers had radios to keep them informed about track conditions up ahead, an express train was barreling toward a station late one stormy night. The station manager was preparing the mail dispatch to be picked up by the train "on the fly." At about 9:30, a man from the nearby town burst into the station office yelling, "The bridge is out! The bridge is out!"

Heavy rains had washed out the railroad bridge no more than a quarter mile past the station. The station master knew that if the train started onto that bridge, disaster was certain. He also knew there was no way to get a message to the engineer. By the time the train got to his station, it would never be able to stop before reaching the bridge.

The station master did the only thing he could think of that might work. He grabbed a lantern and started running up the tracks, toward the oncoming train. "If I can just get a half mile or so up the track, waving my lantern," he thought, "maybe he'll be able to stop in time."

After running 300 yards, the station master was gasping for breath. After 400 yards, he was stumbling along the track, barely able to keep his balance. He could hear the train in the distance, rushing forward. He raced as hard as he could for another 100 yards, but then he stumbled and fell! The lantern flew from his hand and smashed on the ground.

The station master scrambled to his feet, waved his arms, and screamed uselessly in the dark as he watched the train speed past on its way to destruction.

That's the story of so many relationships. The foundation of trust has been removed. The bridge is out. They go speeding by in the night, on their way to ruin.

You may have heard the story about a monastery in Europe that was perched on a cliff hundreds of feet in the air. The only way up was in a large basket tied to a rope. Several monks at the top would haul you up, tugging and pulling with all their strength. Obviously, the ride up that cliff, swinging in the basket, was terrifying.

One day a tourist got extremely nervous about halfway up when he noticed the rope was old and frail. Voice trembling, he asked the monk who was riding with him, "How often do you change the rope?"

The monk thought for a minute and then answered, "Whenever it breaks!"

Sometimes that's too late, isn't it? Trust has to be maintained and repaired constantly. Loving hearts know that and work to keep their personal integrity and the integrity of their relationships.

The Nature of Honesty

How can we tell what our true nature is like? Well, most of us seem to have two natures that are at least slightly different. One we show in public—at work, at church, in social gatherings. The other comes out in private, when no one else is around to see. And that private nature is the true one, the real us. Honesty is what we do in the dark. Someone has said "Character is revealed by what we do in secret."

Honesty comes from within. So it stands to reason that when we lose our integrity, when we break down morally, that also starts within. The crumbling begins there, and then the devil brings temptation into our lives, and we fall.

The people of ancient China, fearing the barbarous tribes to the north, built the Great Wall that's still a popular tourist attraction. It was so thick that nothing could break through it, so high that nothing could climb over it. Then they relaxed to enjoy their security.

In spite of the wall, however, China was invaded from the north three times in the next 100 years. How could that happen? Did the invaders find a way to break through or climb over the wall? No, each time they merely bribed a gatekeeper, then marched through the gate as if the wall wasn't even there.

That's just the way it is with you and me. Moral rot begins within, and then the enemy is able to take over.

One of the best statements I've ever come across was made by Madame Chiang Kai-shek, wife of the late Taiwanese leader. She said, "If the past has taught us anything, it is that every cause brings its effect, and every action has its consequences." That thought is, in my opinion, the moral foundation of the universe. Life keeps books on us all, and we are the sum total of our words and actions. Character can't be counterfeited, nor can it be put on and cast off at the whim of the moment like a garment. Each day we write our destinies, whether we're people of honesty—people of our word who do what we say—or people who can't be trusted.

The temptation is strong to be dishonest in order to gain some kind of advantage. As they say, nothing increases a man's golf score like a witness! But the only way you and I will ever feel good about ourselves is if we're able to trust ourselves and be honest with ourselves and others—if we're the same people in the dark as we are when seen by the rest of the world.

That kind of honesty takes courage sometimes, courage of the sort shown by Dr. Stockmann in Ibsen's play "An Enemy of the People." He was the medical supervisor of the mineral baths in a resort town, and he discovered that the baths were polluted and potentially dangerous.

When he reported that to the town's leaders, they naturally feared financial disaster if the word got out. So Dr. Stockmann's brother, the mayor, told him to retract his findings. The doctor refused, and his brother threatened to fire him.

At that point, Dr. Stockmann went home to talk things over with his wife. She also urged him to retract his findings, to think of his family lest they lose their source of income. At that point, their two young sons came into the room, and the doctor became more convinced than ever that he had to take the risk to be a person of integrity. He turned to his wife and said, "I want to be able to look my boys in the face when they grow up into free men."

Having made up his mind, he went off to do what he had to

do, knowing he would lose his job and be rejected by his fellow townspeople.

He was kind of like the preacher in the cartoon who stood in the pulpit with his suitcase and all his boxes stacked up next to him and said, "Today's sermon is one I've been wanting to preach for a long time."

Integrity of character is so important to who and what we are that when we lose it, we've really lost just about everything. When we lose wealth, that hurts. When we lose health, we've lost a lot. But when we lose character, all is gone.

> "The word is 'integrity'."

The American General Dean, during the Korean War, was captured by the Communists. They put him in a room with a pen and paper and told him he had only a few minutes to write his last letter to his family. Assuming he was about to be executed, he addressed his wife and son, Billy. And the only thing he said to Billy was "tell Bill the word is *integrity*." That says it all. The last words of a condemned man were that the essence of life is integrity, and he was right.

Just what is integrity? The word comes from the mathematical term "integer", a number that hasn't been divided into fractions. It's a whole number. And a person with integrity is a man or woman whose life is not divided against itself, who enjoys wholeness and completeness.

The word "salvation" also derives from a root meaning of "wholeness" or "oneness." So a life of integrity is one that's not fractured and fragmented. You don't *think* one thing, *believe* one thing and *do another*. There's no hypocrisy, no inner warfare like so many people experience. Instead, there's extra energy, power, wellness and clarity of thought.

Unfortunately, examples of the *lack* of integrity can be found in abundance. From comedy comes the story of a man who was sitting reading the morning paper, and his wife sat next to him, reading another section and drinking her coffee.

"Look here in the paper," the man said. "The clerk at our bank stole $100,000 and the bank limousine and ran off with the president's wife."

The woman looked up from her paper and said, "That's terrible! I wonder who's going to teach his Sunday school class this week?"

We don't know whether to laugh or cry when we hear those stories because things like that are really happening all around us. But that kind of double life is unthinkable to people of integrity, people with loving hearts.

Honesty Pays

Honesty obviously pays off in our families. But it also pays off in business. People will shun a company that deals dishonestly, but they'll be drawn to one with integrity.

Donald Douglas built a reputation for great honesty in his aircraft company, and he did everything he could to preserve it. At one point, he was competing with Boeing to sell Eastern Airlines its first jets. Eddie Rickenbacker, who founded and still ran Eastern at that time, told Douglas that his specifications and claims for his DC-8 were close to his competition on everything but noise level. He then gave Douglas one last chance to out-promise Boeing in that regard.

After consulting with his engineers, Douglas reported back that he couldn't make that promise in good conscience.

Rickenbacker replied, "I knew you couldn't. I just wanted to see if you were still honest. You've won yourself an order for $135 million of jets."

Believe it or not, honesty can even pay in politics. Harry Emerson Fosdick told of the time when Abraham Lincoln was warned by his friends not to make a certain speech while campaigning for the Senate in 1858. Lincoln answered, "If it is decreed that I should go down because of this speech, then let me go down linked to the truth." Lincoln actually lost that election, but in the process he made a name for himself, and two years later he became president of the United States.

Don't you wish we had more politicians today with that commitment to the truth?

Honesty will also pay in winning the affection of those whose love is worth having. A true story coming out of World War II, as related by King Duncan in Seven Worlds Publishing, illustrates that beautifully. John Blanchard was a young soldier in basic training in Florida, and one evening he went to the base library. There he found a book to read, and in the margins were notes written in a female hand. They showed insight, understanding and a bit of tenderness.

Blanchard flipped to the front of the book and found the name of its previous owner, a Miss Hollis Maynell. After doing some research, he found her address in New York. He wrote her a letter, and then the next day he was shipped overseas.

For 13 months, the two corresponded, gradually opening their hearts to each other and realizing they were falling in love. He asked her to send a picture of herself, but she refused, saying, "If you really loved me, it wouldn't matter what I looked like."

Finally, the day came when they were to see each other for the first time. They arranged to meet at Grand Central Station in New York at 7 p.m. Hollis told John, "You'll recognize me by the red rose I'll be wearing on my lapel."

As the clock approached 7 o'clock, Blanchard stood at the appointed place, his heart pounding. He noticed a young woman coming toward him, her figure long and sleek, her blonde hair in curls. Her eyes were as blue as flowers, and her lips and chin had an appealing, gentle firmness. Her pale green suit was like springtime come alive.

"I started toward her," Blanchard wrote later, "entirely forgetting to notice that she was not wearing a rose. And as she moved toward me, a smile curled her lips and she said, 'Going my way, soldier?' Almost unconsciously, I stepped closer to her.

"And then," Blanchard wrote, "I saw Hollis Maynell close behind the other girl. A woman well past 40, she had graying hair that was showing under a worn hat. She was more than plump, and her thick-ankled feet were thrust in low-heeled shoes. But she wore a red rose on the lapel of her brown coat.

"The girl in green was walking away. I felt as though I was split in two by the desire to follow her and yet that deep longing for the woman whose spirit had communicated and been with my spirit. And there she stood. Her pale, plump face was gentle and sensitive. Her gray eyes had a warm and timely look, and I did not hesitate. My fingers gripped that small, worn book that was to identify me to her. This might not be love, but it might be more precious than love—a friendship for which I'd been more than grateful.

"I squared my shoulders and saluted and held out the book to that woman, even though while I spoke I felt choked back by the bitterness of my disappointment. 'I'm Lieutenant John Blanchard. You must be Miss Maynell. I'm so glad you could meet me. May I take you to dinner?'

"And the woman's face broadened in a tolerant smile. 'I don't know what this is all about, son,' she answered, 'but the young lady in the green suit who just went by begged me to wear this rose on my coat. And she said that if you were to ask me out to dinner, I should tell you that she is waiting for you in the big restaurant. She said it was some kind of test.' "

John Blanchard passed his test of integrity and honesty. Would you pass a similar test?

Stick to the truth, and you don't have to remember so much. Follow the rules, and decent people will side with you rather than against you. Love the truth, and people will have a hard time controlling you—you give them no leverage. In the real world, honesty is still the best policy.

Finally, honesty pays in the healing it brings to our lives. Whatever is awry emotionally or in relationships, any recovery absolutely has to start with honesty. No friend, loved one or even professional counselor can help those who will not become truthful with themselves and face the facts.

I teach college students, and you can't believe the "smoke" they sometimes blow me. I tell them, "Hey, you can tell that to someone else! I coached for 20 years, and I've already forgotten better excuses than that!"

Occasionally, I give two assignments at the same time, and someone will come in on the due day and say, "I worked hard last night until about three in the morning and just didn't have time to finish!" Of course, I can tell the ones that are blowing smoke instead of being honest with me. How can I, or anyone, help a person who won't tell the truth?

"If we confess our sins," wrote the apostle John, God is faithful and just to forgive and cleanse us (1 John 1:9). Spiritual healing also starts with confession, with facing the facts about ourselves. God certainly knows the truth about us—there's no pulling the wool over His eyes. The sooner we admit the truth and agree with His assessment of it, the better off we'll be.

Perhaps it will help us to be honest if we realize that while honesty pays, lies always cost us, sooner or later. Two high school students got spring fever one beautiful morning, so they skipped class and had a big time. Then they went in that afternoon and told the teacher, "Sorry we're so late. We had a flat tire on the way to school."

The teacher, who knew it was a con job, smiled and said, "That's fine. No problem. You missed a test this morning, but that's OK. I'll let you make it up right now. Just take separate seats."

Once they were seated, the teacher smiled again and continued, "All right, question number one: Which tire went flat?"

Perhaps you've heard about the butcher who was visited by a lady wanting to buy a chicken. He reached into his case, pulled out a chicken, put it on the scale, and gave her the poundage and the price. "You know," she said, "that's really a little smaller chicken than I think I might need. Do you have a larger one?"

That was in fact the only chicken he had at the moment. Rather than admit that, however, he took the bird and reached into his case again, bumbled around for a minute, made a little racket, and then pulled out the same chicken. But this time, when he put it on the scale, he also put his thumb up there before he gave her a new weight and price.

The woman thought about it for a moment, and finally, she said, "You know, that'll be good. In fact, I believe I'll just take both of them."

Sometimes our lies are found out sooner rather than later, but none of them escape detection forever. And when they're found out, we lose in a big way.

For Our Children

As stated earlier, integrity is the foundation of character and the base of all good relationships. If there's one thing we need to teach our children, it's honesty. There's nothing more important we can instill if we want them to have successful, fulfilling lives. Loving hearts know that and so make it a top priority.

How do we teach it? Not so much by what we say as by what we do. We teach it by example.

In the story of Dr. Stockmann from the play "An Enemy of the People," his courageous stand for the truth gave his sons an unforgettable example of being honest regardless of the cost. What kind of regard for truth will they have as they mature?

On the other hand, what kind of lesson do you think is learned by those children whose parents tell them to answer the door or the phone with the lie that they're not home? What do kids learn when they look young enough to qualify for discount tickets, so their parents continue to ask for them even after the kids are too old? These may seem like small things to us, but they teach big, lasting lessons to our children.

In light of that reality, let's resolve that rather than pull our children and grandchildren down with a heritage of lies, big or small, we'll let them grow on our shoulders so they can stand tall, knowing Mom and Dad have always been committed to the truth. There's no better way we can demonstrate loving hearts, and there's no better way we can help our children develop loving hearts.

The great apostle Paul said, "I strive always to keep my conscience clear before God and man" (Acts 24:16). May that be our goal and determination as well.

Chapter Reflection

"Love does not delight in evil, but rejoices in the truth." What does it mean to "rejoice in the truth"?

Discussion Questions

1. Do you agree that dishonesty is a pervasive problem in our country? Explain and give examples.
2. Discuss the growing problem of "white collar crime."
3. In Matthew 5:6(NASB), Christ said, "Blessed are those who hunger and thirst for righteousness, they shall be satisfied." Do you know anyone who you would say was hungry for righteousness? What about yourself?
4. Read Romans 12:2 and Psalms 119:10. What are some ways we can gradually become conformed to the world and not even realize it?

10

Always Optimistic

The pessimist sees the difficulty in every opportunity; the optimist sees the opportunity in every difficulty.
(L. P. Jacks)

Dr. Joe Harding tells the story of a Dr. McDonald who was a prisoner of war in Germany during World War II. He learned about Normandy and D-Day while being held there. Early one morning, another American came in and shook him awake. "The Scotsman wants to see you right away," the man said.

McDonald went over to the barbed-wire fence separating the British and American prisoners, and the Scotsman simply told him, "They have come! They have come!"

Back in the American barracks, McDonald started screaming, running around, and telling everybody, "They've come! They've come! They've come!" At that, all the men started shouting, hugging each other and crying. Then they ran out in the street and rolled in the dirt with joy.

The German guards watching them must have thought they were crazy. And why not? Nothing physical had changed. The Americans were still prisoners at the mercy of their Nazi captors.

What had changed, however, was that suddenly the Americans had *hope*. Allied troops were on their way. Freedom was in sight, a certainty only weeks or even days away. That hope made all the difference.

A lady named Ruele Howe tells about growing up in the country and about how, when she was 15 years old, her house burned down. The family members escaped with nothing but the clothes on their backs.

Since there were no neighbors nearby, she and her father had to walk to the village to try and get some help. When they returned, they saw something that stayed with Ruele all her days. Beside the charred remains of what had been their home, her mother had laid out a little lunch on a log, and next to it was a tiny can filled with wildflowers.

Those flowers were a symbol of hope, of optimism, of a love of life in the midst of tragedy. They were a statement that no matter what happens, they will always face the future confidently because they know it's in the hands of a Lord who loves them. "[Love] . . . always trusts, always hopes" (1 Corinthians 13:7).

Lucille Ball once said, "One of the things I learned the hard way was that it does not pay to get discouraged. Keeping busy and making optimism a way of life can restore your faith in yourself." Optimism and hope are built out of a loving, Godlike heart.

There are basically just two kinds of human beings. Some think of life as a privilege, while the rest think of it as an endless string of problems. And that difference in outlook has a big impact. The first are enthusiastic, energetic people who love a challenge and are resilient in the face of pain and sickness. They see life as hopeful and exciting. The other people—the pessimists—are hesitant, suspicious and self-centered. To them, life is just a possible ambush.

Benjamin Reeves tells about a little boy whose mother had died, so his father was trying to be both mother and father to him. And under those difficult circumstances, the dad had scheduled a picnic for them.

The boy had never been on a picnic, and he was so excited the night before that he couldn't sleep. Soon, there was a patter of little feet down the hall to the bedroom where his father was sleeping. He shook his dad, who would have responded gruffly except that he saw the expression on his child's face.

"What's the matter, Son?" he said.

"Oh, Daddy," he answered, "tomorrow's going to be such a wonderful day! I just can't sleep, I'm so excited!"

The dad laughed and said, "Well, it won't be a wonderful day if you don't get some sleep. Now you go back to your bedroom and try to sleep."

You've already guessed the next part of the story. A little while later, the sound of small feet echoed down the hall again. The father was sleeping soundly when the boy came in and shook his shoulder excitedly.

> *"I just want to thank you for tomorrow."*

"What do you want now, Son?" the man said.

"Daddy," the boy told him, "I just want to thank you for tomorrow."

That's the kind of excitement and optimism we can have in the Christian life. We just want to thank God for the hope we have both here and in the future because of who He is, what He has promised us and the way He has proved Himself worthy of our trust.

Think of Abraham back in the book of Genesis. God told him to leave his country and his relatives and go to a land he had never seen, and there He would make of him a great nation (Genesis 12:1-3). Abraham was already an old man and had no children. If he obeyed, he would have no homeland and no extended family. And God was promising he'd be a father of nations?

But Paul told us that "against all hope, Abraham in hope believed and so became the father of many nations, just as it had been said to him" (Romans 4:18). He believed in God's promises and found them to be true and reliable. And so will we if we follow His leading the way Abraham did.

Jesus was probably the greatest optimist who ever lived. Why? Because He knew the outcome of His life. He knew what the Father had promised and ordained, and He had a hope built on absolute trust that all would work out to His glory in the end.

"Let us fix our eyes on Jesus," said the writer to the Hebrews, "the author and perfecter of our faith, *who for the joy set before him endured the cross*, scorning its shame, and sat down at the right hand of the throne of God" (Hebrews 12:2, emphasis added). He had that sure hope, a perfect illustration of Hebrews 11:1: "Now faith is being sure of what we hope for and certain of what we do not see."

With the same confidence, Jesus said in Matthew 16:18, "I will build my church, and the gates of Hades will not overcome it." He was looking ahead through thousands of years of church history yet to be written, but He was doing so with trust in the plan and promises of the Father.

Because we have the same Father, we can have the same hope in His good will for us. Romans 8:28 is not just a warm blanket to comfort those who are hurting but a solid rock on which we can build an attitude and a life: "And we know that in all things God works for the good of those who love him, who have been called according to his purpose."

Like Jesus, we know the ultimate, God-glorifying end of all things. It's recorded in God's Word. And the bottom line is this, from Jesus Himself: "In this world you will have trouble. But take heart! I have overcome the world" (John 16:33). So we, too, can be optimistic based on the sure hope that all is ultimately in His hands.

"Praise be to the God and Father of our Lord Jesus Christ!" Peter wrote. "In his great mercy he has given us new birth into a living hope through the resurrection of Jesus Christ from the dead, and into an inheritance that can never perish, spoil or fade—kept in heaven for you, who through faith are shielded by God's power until the coming of the salvation that is ready to be revealed in the last time" (1 Peter 1:3-5). Ours is a living hope because of what Jesus and the Father have done.

Accept No Substitutes

Within the last couple of decades, some researchers were promising that Laetrile, a drug extracted from apricot pits, would cure cancer of every type without negative side effects. Thousands of cancer sufferers, desperate for healing and unable to find a U.S. doctor to administer the treatments, journeyed to Mexico full of hope.

Eventually, however, studies by the National Cancer Institute found that Laetrile treatments not only did no good, but they could actually be harmful and often were. Many patients, the doctors said, were killed by their hope in a worthless treatment used in place of another that might have done some good.

> *It's not so much a question of how much hope we have but in what we hope. When the facts won't budge, your attitude must bend.*

That's a simple illustration in the physical world of the kind of bogus hope to which so many people cling. We all need hope—we can't live without it. As Martin Luther once wrote, everything that's done in this world is done by hope. Or, as Orson Sweat Martin put it, "There's no medicine like hope, no incentive so great and no tonic so powerful as expectation of something better tomorrow."

But we need a solid, genuine hope. It's not so much a question of *how much* hope we have but *in what* we hope. And real hope comes through the resurrection, life and power of Jesus Christ.

A needle on a compass will tremble as it seeks to find the North Pole. A flower lifts its drooping head toward the sun's powerful rays. But a 59-cent magnet will also attract the compass needle, and a flower can grow under the heat and light of a lamp's bulb.

Wouldn't it be sad, though, if that compass knew only the tiny magnet pull and never felt the great pull of the North Pole? Wouldn't it be a shame if that flower only knew the heat from the lightbulb and never the sun's warmth? So it is with our lives if we know only the cheap imitations of God's hope and optimism.

What would the world have us hope in? In money and our ability to make it. In an ever-growing pile of possessions. In our physical attractiveness. In our intelligence or in the degrees earned or in our professional credentials. In our ability to attract members of the opposite sex.

But all those things can be taken away. And even if they're not, in the tough times of life, their emptiness becomes painfully obvious. The world simply has no good substitute for the real hope that only God can offer.

The ultimate test of any source of hope is what it means to us when we reach life's final threshold. Will any of the world's sources help us then? No, that's when their futility is most obvious of all. But compare that with the solid, biblical hope expressed by Warren Chandler as he lay dying. Friends came and asked him, "Do you dread crossing the river of death?"

Smiling weakly, he answered, "My father owns the land on both sides of the river. Why should I be afraid?" This hope in Christ affects our attitude toward dying. Henry Van Dyke expresses it beautifully:

> I am standing upon the seashore. A ship at my side spreads her white sails to the morning breeze and starts for the blue ocean. She is an object of beauty and strength, and I stand and watch her until at lengh she hangs like a speck of white cloud just where the sea and

sky come down to mingle with each other. Then someone at my side says: "There! She's gone."

Gone where? Gone from my sight—that is all. She is just as large in mast and hull and spar as she was when she left my side, and just as able to bear her load of living freight to the place of destination. Her diminished size is in me—not in her; and just at the moment when someone at my side says, "There! She's gone," there are other eyes watching her coming, and other voices ready to take up the glad shout, "There she comes!"

And that is dying.

Realistic Hope

When I say loving hearts are optimistic, please don't understand me to say we should have a Pollyanna-type of mindset that ignores the difficult realities of life. I'm not suggesting we should say everything is wonderful when it clearly is not. We have to accept and deal with life as it's handed to us.

The fact is that there are some things we'll never be able to change, as much as we'd like to. But we *must* find a productive and upbuilding way to handle our relationships with difficult people and situations.

Dr. Barker, a one-time White House physician, said he asked the happiest man he'd ever known, in St. Louis, "How in the world do you manage to be so happy?"

"Well, I'll tell you a story," his friend answered. "When I was a young man, I fell head-over-heels in love with the sweetest girl, and she still is and I still am. We've been married for 40 years now.

"But she had one fault then, and she still does. She's always been late for things. One time when we were dating, she begged me to take her to the concert of this certain singer. And I promised her that if she would be ready 30 minutes before the concert, I would get the tickets and take her.

"Well, I went over to her place even earlier than that. Her mother invited me in and said, 'Nellie will never be ready in time. She just came in.'

"I stood there a minute and then began to pace up and

down the floor, getting more and more angry by the minute as I watched the clock. Sure enough, the 30-minute deadline passed. I just sat down on a chair in the hall in frustration.

"Beside me on a table was a book. I opened it, and on the flyleaf were written three sentences that changed my life. Here's what they said: 'For every evil under the sun, there is a remedy or there is none. If there's one, seek till you find it. If there's none, never mind it.'

"I decided in that moment that I couldn't change Nellie's habit of tardiness, and I decided to accept it. I did that with everything in my life I couldn't change, and it's brought me the greatest joy and happiness."

There will always be difficult and even painful circumstances we can't change. The only thing we *can* change—we are in fact responsible to change it—is our attitude and response to those people and situations. In the last chapter we explored our need to be honest with ourselves. That includes accepting the fact that we're responsible for our attitude and how we handle what life brings our way.

Go to a prison and ask the inmates why they're there. You'll hear things like "I was framed." "They ganged up on me." "Mistaken identity." "The police had it in for me." Very few will say, "I was guilty." And they have no realistic hope of overcoming their problems and making something of their lives until they accept the reality of what they've done and their responsibility for it.

An insurance adjustor said that in his estimation, "90 percent of all the people I'm involved with in accident investigations see themselves as blameless." How many of them do you think will become better drivers as a result of their accidents?

Will Rogers said there were three phases of American history: the passing of the Indian, the passing of the buffalo and the passing of the buck. Sooner or later, if we're going to be happy based on a realistic hope for the future, we've got to take responsibility for ourselves.

I remember one year when we were planning a Christmas party at Hamby, where I preach. I went down to the restaurant to pick up the turkey and dressing. When we ordered, I specifically requested the meat and dressing to be put in individual servings for the buffet dinner.

When I got there, I found the turkey was in one big pan, with the dressing in another. I immediately reacted, saying, "This isn't the way I ordered this."

"Well, let's see the ticket," the man said. He looked it up and found that I was right. "OK," he went on, "if you have time to wait, we can prepare individual servings for you."

"No," I said, "I don't have time to wait." And then it suddenly occurred to me, "This is reality, this moment, and I can't change it. This is just the way it is."

So I changed my attitude and said, "Oh, this will be all right. I'll take it just like this. It may work out better anyway."

When I did that, the response from the man was unbelievable. He visited with me as he helped me load everything in my car and gave me all the things I needed. The next day, when I returned some of the utensils, he met me with a smile and told me again how much he appreciated my response to the mix-up and how few people react positively to a mix-up.

Then it occurred to me that while I was accepting reality in a positive way the day before, something bigger and deeper had also been taking place. You see, that guy knew where I was from and that I represent Christianity. It would have been a shame if I had blown it with my attitude in that encounter. And I almost did!

Every Christian represents Christ to the rest of the world all day long, every day. We can't change difficult realities any more than an unbeliever can, but we can change the way we accept and respond to them.

I like the attitude of a man described by Arthur Gordon when he reported on the status of the U.S. Eighth Air Force in England during World War II. "There in the countryside it was like a sea of mud," Gordon wrote, "and the people were cold and miserable and homesick. They were being shot at, and morale was low."

But, he continued, "There was one sergeant, a crew chief, who was always cheerful, always had a good sense of humor, always smiling." One day, Gordon watched him struggle in a freezing rain to salvage a flying fortress that had slid off a runway into what seemed like a bottomless pit of mire. In spite of the conditions, the airman was whistling like a lark.

Gordon approached and said to him, "How can you whistle in a mess like this?"

The sergeant, with a mud-cake grin, answered, "When the facts won't budge, you have to bend your attitude to fit them. That's all."

Isn't that good advice? We can't change some things, but we can bend our attitude to make the most of the situation, knowing Romans 8:28 and all of God's other promises are still in effect.

Optimism's Fruit

The most obvious sign of an optimistic attitude is a warm, genuine smile. But it works the other way, too—smiling makes us feel better and helps us have a better outlook. It actually changes the chemistry of the body. As someone said, we don't smile because we're happy—we're happy because we smile. So let's smile. Let's allow people to see the optimism God has put in our hearts and show them our hearts are at home. It will be like sunshine playing around our lips.

Did you ever notice that smiling is one of the first things children learn how to do? An optimist laughs to forget; a pessimist forgets to laugh. An honest, beautiful smile is one of the best gifts we can give someone; yet, it costs nothing. It takes only a fleeting moment to deliver, but the memory can last a lifetime. It's the one thing we can wear that will never go out of style; it is, in fact, the most important thing we can wear.

The Value of A Smile

It costs nothing, but creates much.

It enriches those who receive without impoverishing those who give.

Always Optimistic

It happens in a flash, and the memory of it sometimes lasts forever.

None are so rich they can get along without it, and none so poor but are richer for its benefits.

It creates happiness in the home, fosters goodwill in a business and is the countersign of friends.

It is rest to the weary, daylight to the discouraged, sunshine to the sad and nature's best antidote for trouble.

Yet, it cannot be bought, begged, borrowed or stolen, for it is something that is no earthly good to anyone until it is given away.
—Author Unknown

Whether we're optimistic or pessimistic about the future affects our health, too. Studies have shown our attitude has a profound impact on the immune system. Placebos—sugar pills—work between 30 and 60 percent of the time, helping sick people get better, simply because they *think* they're getting medicine and so *expect* the pills to work. Pessimists, on the other hand, seem to have less resistance to disease, so they get sick more often.

Obviously, our attitude also affects us socially. Hopeful, optimistic people are just more fun to be around. They're more friendly and so have more friends. Pessimists who think others won't like them tend to create self-fulfilling prophecies.

What's not quite so obvious is that our attitude also affects our success in business. Optimistic people do better than their equally talented but pessimistic counterparts, no matter what the field. The Metropolitan Life insurance company, for example, has found that optimists outsell pessimists by 20 percent in the first year and by 50 percent the following year.

Finally, optimism can also help us spiritually. We could all learn from a story by Patt Barnes about an old flower lady who sat on the street corner wearing a beautiful smile on her wrinkled face. She was alive with joy. One day a man approached her and said, "My, you look happy this morning."

"Why not?" she responded. "Everything's good."

She was shabbily dressed and obviously poor, so the man asked, "Well, don't you have any troubles?"

"Oh," she said, "you can't reach my age and not have troubles, but it's like Jesus and the resurrection. When Jesus was crucified on that Friday, that was the worst day in the whole world. And when I get troubles, I remember that day. But then I think of what happened three days later—resurrection. The Lord came forth. So when things go wrong, I've just learned to wait three days, and somehow every time things get much better."

When we have trust in God and His love for us, we can be patient and give Him a chance to help. Pessimists frankly don't expect much from Him. But we'll see Him do a lot more, and we'll grow a lot more in our faith, when we offer Him that opportunity to show Himself faithful.

Fear knocked at the door but when faith answered, no one was there. Loving hearts know the excitement of optimism, the power of hope and the peace of trust in a loving Lord.

Chapter Reflection

As quoted in the chapter, Lucille Ball said, "One of the things I learned the hard way was that it does not pay to get discouraged." What do you think she meant? In what ways is discouragement self-defeating? (Note Proverbs 12:25: "Anxiety in the heart of a man weighs it down, But a good word makes it glad."

Discussion Questions

1. What does it mean to be optimistic? Does it mean to ignore problems, hoping they will go away? Does it mean to overlook or disregard obstacles in your way? Explain.

2. Psalms 105:3 says, "Glory in His holy name; Let the heart of those who see the Lord be glad." Should religious people be glad and joyful? Is it realistic to expect Christians to always be optimistic? Is it sinful to be a pessimist?

3. How can a person become more optimistic? What can you say to someone who is discouraged or has become a pessimist?

4. Can John 15:11 and a life of pessimism go together?

11
Willingness to Persevere

> *If you're ever tempted to give up, just think of Brahms who took seven long years to compose his famous Lullaby. Keep falling asleep at the piano."*
> (Robert Orben)

When I was in junior college, we didn't have an athletic program. We had one of those special days when the girls would cheer and the boys would run. We also had a literal Cow Bowl, where we'd try to run from one end of the field to the other without stepping in something.

Some of us laid out a 440-yard track, and then a bunch of us lined up to run. We started off, and I was pumping my old long legs pretty well. Going into the backstretch, I was in second place. Then it was into the final curve, where those monkeys jump on your back—I got a gorilla coming out of there!

As we finished that curve, I pulled up beside the leader, a short and speedy friend named Davis. We were running side by side, but I tired and dropped back, still in second place. Starting into the home stretch, however, I pushed myself and pulled even again. We were neck and neck as we approached the finish line.

At the very last, though, I tired again and dropped to second as Davis won. Still, I felt pretty good about how I had done—until Davis came up to me and said, "Boy, Willard, I'll tell you, if you'd have pushed me one more time, I'd have given up."

If only I had known, right? If only I had realized just how close I was to winning, I'd have found that last burst of energy. But I didn't know, and we can't know in life's struggles how close we are to victory.

Elbert Hubbard put it this way:

> The line between failure and success is so fine that we scarcely know when we pass it; so fine that we are often on the line and do not know it. How many a man has thrown up his hands at a time when a little more effort, a little more patience, would have achieved success. As the tide goes clear out, so it comes clear in.
>
> Sometimes, prospects may seem darkest when really they are on the turn. A little more persistence, a little more effort, and what seemed hopeless failure may turn to glorious success. There is no failure except in no longer trying. There is no defeat except from within, no really insurmountable barrier save our own inherent weakness of purpose.

It's so important in every area of our lives to develop a willingness to persevere. "[Love] . . . always perseveres" (1 Corinthians 13:7).

> *We never know how close we are to victory.*

After surviving 54 hours adrift in the Atlantic Ocean off the coast of South Carolina some time back, a man said, "I just can't take it anymore" and jumped off the life raft to his death. Only an hour later, the Coast Guard spotted the raft and sent a rescue ship. Had he only known how close he was, he could have found the strength to endure.

In a humorous vein, Victor Borge tells about his uncle who wanted to invent a new soft drink. He worked on a formula for a number of years and called it 4 Up. It failed. He went back to the lab, worked and worked, and came up with another formula he called 5 Up. It didn't succeed, either. He went back again and worked some more and came up with, you guessed it, 6 Up.

Exhausted and disgusted, he gave up and quit. "What a shame," Borge says. "He never knew how close he came!"

Too Early to Quit

Stories like that make it clear that it's always too early to quit. We need to fight one more round, keep on keeping on. It really doesn't matter how many times we stumble or fail if we'll always get up just one more time. The only time we have to succeed at something is the last time we try.

Richard Hooker spent 17 long years writing a funny story about the Korean War. After all that time and effort, he sent it to 21 different publishers and received 21 rejection letters in reply. But did he give up in despair? No, he sent it out one more time.

That publisher, William Morrow, accepted the book and published it as *M*A*S*H*. And the rest, as they say, is history. Whether you like the book or not, Hooker's persistence is a model worthy of being imitated.

The flip side of the coin is seen in the lives of the people who inhabit skid row. Researchers have found that those people come from very different backgrounds and circumstances. There's a lot they don't have in common. But the one thing they all share is that they've given up on life.

> A graceful child my pathway crossed
> As late I trod the busy street,
> And slightly over her head she tossed
> A rope which swiftly passed her feet.
> I, in her presence, took a part,
> And when she paused I said to her,
> "How did you learn that pretty art?"
> And she answered, "I kept trying, sir."
> —Author Unknown

I started coaching college basketball when I wasn't "dry behind the ears." We started on a dirt court with no players, no scholarships, no schedule and no coach, either—I just didn't know it! I actually thought I was pretty good. If I had known how little I really knew, I probably would have quit.

Instead, though, I endured the lopsided losses and just kept with it. The result was we became a respectable contender with a good program in good facilities. As a result of that success, I was recommended for and accepted the head coaching position at a four-year college. My success was not due to any brilliance on my part but to simple persistence. I never gave up.

> *The only time we have to succeed is the last time we try.*

Second Corinthians 4:8, in the Easy-to-Read version, translates Paul this way: "We often don't know what to do, but we never give up." He was referring to his life's mission of spreading the Gospel, motivated by love for the Savior and for lost souls, and his life was indeed a testimony to perseverance.

Enemies plotted to kill him in Damascus, Ephesus, Corinth and Jerusalem. They drove him out of Antioch and Berea and tried to stone him in Iconium. They did stone him in Lystra, leaving him for dead. In Philippi, they beat him with rods and put him in stocks. They tried to mob him in Thessalonica.

Along the way, Paul also was shipwrecked, often hungry, bitten by a serpent and unjustly imprisoned for years. Finally, according to tradition, he was executed for his faith. That was his final victory!

He never gave up, and he started and nurtured churches throughout the known world of his time. He also left behind some of the most important doctrinal teaching in the New Testament. Today, his name and work live on, being used greatly by the Holy Spirit. His enemies, on the other hand, have long been forgotten.

I don't think there's any question but that persistence is the single greatest factor to success in any field. Calvin Coolidge said it this way:

> Nothing in this world can take the place of persistence. Talent will not; nothing is more common than unsuccessful men with talent. Genius will not; unrewarded genius is almost a proverb. Education will not; the world is full of educated derelicts. Persistence and determination alone are omnipotent. The slogan "press on" has solved and always will solve the problems of the human race.

"Press on," with God's help, solves more problems than anything else. Impatient people start things, but patient people finish them with persistence. No matter what field you consider—a line of work, a marriage, a ministry in the church—persistence is the biggest key to success.

The story is told of the Mongol emperor Tamerlane, whose army was defeated and scattered in every direction on one occasion. Tamerlane himself had to hide in an old barn to escape his enemies. While he was there, he observed an ant trying to carry off a kernel of corn.

The kernel was far larger than the ant, and the ant had to push it over a wall to get it out of the barn. Needless to say, it was quite a struggle. As the ant got close to the top each time, it would lose its grip on the wall, and it and the kernel would go tumbling back to the bottom.

But the ant never quit. *Sixty-nine times* this sequence of events repeated itself. Sixty-nine times the ant failed. Finally, on the 70th try, the ant succeeded in pushing the kernel over the wall. Tamerlane watched the ant's persistence with admiration and concluded, "If an ant can do it, so can I." And with that model in mind, he went out, reorganized his army and came back to defeat the enemy and build an empire.

I can think of so many people who had great beginnings but never finished, never persisted. It is a sad thing to see a good beginning but a bad ending. The Bible is full of such examples. Think of King Saul, Judas, Solomon and the whole nation of Israel. Jesus said, "No one who puts his hand to the plow and looks back is fit for service in the kingdom of God" (Luke 9:62). He also said, "He who stands firm to the end will be saved" (Matthew 10:22).

> *When you get to the end of the rope, tie a knot and hang on.*

On the other hand, love and trust enabled many biblical saints to hang in there. Noah waited 120 years before it rained. Abraham was 100 years old when his son Isaac was born. Joseph served 14 years of false imprisonment before he was vindicated. Moses waited 40 years in the desert before God called him back into service to lead the Exodus.

What we have to realize is that God's timetable does not match our own. He knows far more and far better, and we just can't predict when He will bring things together for good in a way we can recognize. That's why we have to love Him and love life. That love will keep us patiently persisting. And when we get to the end of our rope, we just have to tie a knot and hang on.

Little Things Mean a Lot

Persistence in doing the right things can make such a difference that we don't have to do great feats in order to succeed. We don't have to change everything. None of us is that far off from considerable achievement. As stated earlier, persistence is more important than talent or brains. Little things done right, over time, add up to very big accomplishments.

A certain college professor had taught for about 20 years and watched thousands of students pass through his classes. Then, he began to wonder what had happened to some of those young people, so he did a study.

What he discovered was that his students were much alike in their habits and characteristics. The differences between them were small. However, 20 years after leaving college, there were tremendous differences in their lives and the things they had achieved. The professor kept asking why that was so.

After the study was complete, he reached this conclusion: "There seems to be but little difference between winners and losers, but this little seems to make the difference. All of us seem to be endowed with larger qualities of life, but some possess the single extra heartbeat that often spells the difference between success and failure. There's no thread in life so narrow as the one that divides the winners from the losers."

The little difference might be a few extra hours of work each week, the extra call made, the ability to hold on for perhaps just a single day after others have thrown in the towel, or a commitment to prayer when others are still sleeping. We could make an almost-endless list of such simple little things that become powerful when done with persistence.

Obviously, though, we don't get things done by procrastinating. Putting off good or necessary work until tomorrow is a small thing that, over time, will lead to *lack* of accomplishment and frustration. We can let a task grow into an unclimbable mountain in our imagination; we need to start where we are and how we can. We cannot look for someone else to get the job done; we need to jump in ourselves. Half-hearted effort won't do the trick, either; let's put everything we've got into everything we do. And finally, once we start, let's not quit. Let's persevere to the end.

Persist at What?

For persistence to make sense to a loving heart, the goal in mind has to be a worthy one. In other words, we have to know what's worth staying with. We don't persevere in everything with blind stubbornness, like a bulldog with a toy bone.

We have to know what's important and what merits a lifetime of effort.

That means we need to put some time into thinking through and setting good goals. (This is covered more fully in an earlier book, *How to Get What You Want and Want What You Get*.) As stated in the last chapter, the reality is that life is sometimes very difficult, so if we're going to persist when the going gets tough, when others are dropping by the wayside, we have to know that the goals toward which we're working are worth the effort and will be rewarding in the end.

The people who have good goals and the staying power to go with them make the positive difference in this life. They're the people who wear well. They stay and stay, and those around them are glad they do.

For example, Lord Nelson, the famous English naval hero, surprisingly enough suffered from seasickness much of his life. Yet, he managed to destroy Napoleon's fleet. Talking about overcoming your private war, whatever it might be, he said, "No one will pin a medal on you for winning it, but nothing can ever dim the satisfaction of knowing that you did not surrender."

As Lord Nelson suggested, we shouldn't expect success or acclaim overnight. If that happened, we wouldn't need to persist. People laughed at Noah. They laughed at David and his sling. They laughed at Jesus. They laughed at Galileo and at the man who designed the Golden Gate Bridge.

A key difference between winners and losers is that the winners lose more often. That is, they keep trying, and they keep getting up when they fall. In the final analysis, after all, nobody can really "make" things happen. God is in charge of this universe, not us. But through persistence in pursuing good goals, we put ourselves in a position where good things can happen to us. We learn, we make adjustments, and eventually our persistence pays off in relationships, in business success, or in whatever else we're trying to accomplish.

Choice words on this subject by two men who achieved great success in their chosen fields and who were speaking about their respective lines of work applies just as well to all of us.

Ross Perot, an entrepreneur who built his company into a huge success (a *Fortune 500* company), said his one-sentence advice to fellow entrepreneurs would be this: "Persevere, no matter the pain."

And Thomas Edison, the famous inventor, described his success this way: "I start where the last man left off. He didn't stay long enough."

When loving hearts fix on a goal worthy of their time, effort and prayer, they stay long enough. No matter the pain, they get the job done.

Chapter Reflection

The Bible has much to say about perseverence. In general, what does that say about the path we are to follow as Christians?

Discussion Questions

1. Would you agree that most people start out about the same and that the primary difference between success and failure is perseverence? Explain.

2. Read and reflect on Luke 9:62, 1 Timothy 4:16 and Acts 14:21,22. Summarize the meaning of each of them, putting each verse into your own words.

3. Can perseverence be developed in a person? How?

4. Patience is also often mentioned as a characteristic of God's people. Galatians 5:22 lists patience as one of the fruits of the spirit. Are patience and perseverence linked? Explain.

12

Never Lets Others Down

We should measure affection, not like youngsters by the ardor of its passion, but by its strength and constancy.
(Cicero)

During a seminar once, a man came up to me during a break and said, "I want to tell you a true story." His story was about a man named Frank who came home late from work one night, extremely tired. It had been "one of those days," and his family was out, so he was looking forward to relaxing for a few minutes by himself. Shortly after he got in the door, though, the phone rang.

The caller asked, "Are you the people who have custody of the old hotel downtown?"

"Yes," Frank answered, "we have charge of it."

"Well," the caller said, "my wife and I spent our honeymoon in that hotel, and this is our 50th anniversary. We stayed in room 803, and I wonder if you'd let me go down and get the door plate off that room so I can give it to my wife."

Frank wanted to do anything in the world but get up, put his shoes back on and fight traffic to go downtown again. Nevertheless, he did all that and met the caller at the hotel, now out of business and condemned.

The caller turned out to be well up in his 70s, and they started climbing those eight flights of stairs. Frank said he thought he would end up having to carry the old man, whose knees were giving out. He just hoped they would make it all the way.

When they got to the eighth floor, Frank gave the old man a screwdriver, and he took off the plate on the door. They made it back to the ground floor, and Frank thought he would finally get to go home and rest. But the elderly gentleman said, "Say, have you got a minute?"

"Sure," Frank said with a hint of resignation.

"You know," the old man continued, "my wife and I made a promise that we'd tell each other 'I love you' every day. But we also made an agreement that if we ever got to the place where we couldn't say it, we'd just say '803.' "

That anniversary couple knew that relationships are the key to happiness. Their loving hearts had found a wonderful way to express their affection, helping to forge a bond between them that had only grown stronger through the years.

Solid relationships with God, with others and even with ourselves really are vital to our well-being. So we need to learn to relate before it's too late. And relationships are sustained by a love that never lets others down—the most powerful force in the universe. "Love never fails" (1 Corinthians 13:8).

The Source of Love

Such love comes, of course, from God. First Corinthians 13 is, after all, first and foremost a description of the way He loves. And the wonderful truth is that we don't have to do or be anything special to become the objects of that love. All we have to do is respond and be faithful to it. Love never fails—certainly not God's

Judge Ziglar puts it well. He says that in 1952 he wrecked four cars, three so badly that Lloyd's of London said no one could have survived the crashes. Judge thought at the time, "The Lord must have something for me to do."

In 1972 he had a massive heart attack but survived. He thought again, "God must have something for me to do." In

1974 he had two more massive heart attacks, and once more he thought God must be sparing him for some special purpose. In 1976 he had two more serious operations, and sometime later he was hit head-on by a truck going 80 miles per hour.

Finally, however, sitting at breakfast one day, he had a thought that the Lord seemed to be saying, "It's not necessary for Me to have anything special for you to do. I just love you. I just love you."

Being faithful and responding to that love is part of our overall purpose of bringing glory to Him. But God loves us even when we don't respond as we should—love never fails. Aren't you thankful He has never given up on you or stopped loving you? I know I am. Just as Jesus never gave up on His disciples—weak, slow learners, interested in worldly positions—He never forsakes us.

Another name for this kind of love is *unconditional* love, love that gives without concern for whether it receives anything in return. Someone has said that such love may not make the world go around, but it makes the trip worthwhile.

There's a beautiful family in my home town of Abilene that for years has shown an interest in college athletes and given them a home away from home. One young man became almost like a family member—he still is today.

I was talking with the wife about how they've been able to help him so much, and she said, "Well, we just didn't get upset when he didn't come when he said he would, or when he didn't call to tell us he wasn't coming. We didn't expect anything. We just gave a lot of love."

Isn't that beautiful? What would happen if we treated each other, including our spouses, that way? Isn't giving without expectation of reward what love is all about?

Children are a good reminder of God's love. In our Sunday school class, many of the couples were talking about the preceding week and their experiences with their children and the anxieties and pressures of being parents. One couple, who had no children, was just listening to all the conversations. Finally, the wife spoke up and said, "After hearing all of you talk about your kids, why should my husband and I want any? Why would we want to go through all you're describing?"

I thought that was a good question, so I asked the class, "In one sentence, what do your children mean to you?"

We started around the room, and it turned into a time of testimony. One parent said, "When I look in my children's eyes and they can't say a word, but they're looking back at me and saying 'I love you' with those eyes, it's worth everything in the world."

Another said, "When I think about how much I love my children, then I think about how much God must love me, His child."

Another said, "To hear them call you Mommy is worth it all."

Still another said to a fellow member of the class, "You know, I was in high school with you and you were sort of a rough character. Now, to see you hold your son here in church and to see how much you love him makes the drive worthwhile."

By that time, there wasn't a dry eye in the room. Then one more man spoke about how his wife had been killed in an accident three years earlier, leaving him with three young children, but that she lived on in the looks and traits of their youngest daughter.

When we give love to our children, knowing it will never end even though it may not always be returned, we are reminded of God's love for us. He asked rhetorically in Isaiah 49:15, "Can a mother forget the baby at her breast and have no compassion on the child she has borne?" It's almost unthinkable, but He went on to say, "Though she may forget, I will not forget you!"

Bobbie and I have four beautiful grandchildren, and I think I love them with all my heart. But as much as I care for them, I don't love them like Bobbie does. There's something special about a mother's love. And Isaiah 49:15 says to me that God loves us not only as a father, but also as a mother, with that unique level of care.

Then God went on to say in verse 16, "See, I have engraved you on the palms of my hands." In other words, "Every time I look at My hands I see you—you're tattooed there. I can't see Myself without thinking of you!" That's love that never fails.

Our Need for Love

The world is short on two things—love and joy, the things most people hunger for and will accept anywhere they can be found.

A report on the TV show "60 Minutes" described people who had undergone major heart surgery. Some of them had pets; others didn't. And a follow-up study showed that nearly a third of those who didn't have pets had died within a year of their surgeries. Of those who had pets, however, *only one* had died within a year.

People shouldn't need to get all their love from pets, however. We have the ability as fellow human beings, and especially as Christians, to give people love and to build relationships.

A fable tells of a young girl who was walking through a meadow and saw a butterfly hung on a thorn. She released it, and it started to fly away, but then it came back as a good fairy and said, "For your kindness in releasing me, I'll grant you your fondest wish."

The girl said, "I'd like to be happy."

And so for the rest of her life, no one was happier than she. As she became old, all the neighbors feared that the secret of happiness would die with her, so they begged her to let them in on it. She simply said, "The fairy told me that everybody, no matter how secure they seemed, needed me. They needed me."

As we realize that others need us, we, too, can choose to be givers and builders. The fact is that everyone we meet needs some encouragement, some recognition, maybe something as simple as a smile. And every contact we make affects the other person (and us) either positively or negatively. That motivates me to want to reach out in love, knowing even the smallest gesture helps to meet that need.

No Price Tag

Some commercials run on television, especially before Christmas, really bug me. What they're selling is diamond jewelry, and they always show a man giving his wife an outrageously expensive bauble while the voiceover says, "This year, give her the gift of love—diamonds." What they're suggesting is that in order to *really* love someone, you have to spend a lot of money to show it.

Loving hearts know, however, that you can't put a price tag on love. Money is nice, and giving gifts is great fun, but love isn't bought and sold. You don't need a single cent to show love to others. Love shows itself in self-giving words and actions.

The *New York Daily News* ran an article about a children's museum in Edinburgh, Scotland. It was full of childhood treasures—teddy bears, puppets, rocking horses, model trains, games, books, etc. Cases and cases were stuffed with baby dolls, porcelain dolls, costume dolls and walking, talking, somersaulting dolls—the expensive, onetime playmates of very privileged kids.

Off in one corner of another case, sitting alone, was an old, ragged doll. It began life rough and grew much worse for wear. *Shabby* is a fair description. With the doll was a sign that said, "Doll belonging to London slum child, circa 1905."

The body was made of tattered, brown socks stuffed with rags. The arms were two thin sticks of wood covered with wool. The head was the worn-down, battered heel of a man's shoe, with the nails visible around the edges. The face was small bits of paper pasted on for eyes, nose, and mouth. The hair was a sock, and the clothes were a plain gingham dress and a rough apron. The mouth did not smile.

Some would call the doll ugly, but they would be very wrong. Historians tell us that around 1905, there were no bleaker slums in all the world than those of London. Yet, somewhere in those slums, a tenderhearted mother or father created that doll out of what materials they had and love beyond measure. Seen in that light, the doll was so very pitiful but so very beautiful.

A minister was talking to his Sunday school class of teenagers about things money can and can't buy. "You can't buy laughter," he said. "That comes from the soul. You also can't buy love." Then, to drive his point home, he asked, "What would you do if I offered you a thousand dollars not to love your mother or father?"

A moment of silence followed as the boys and girls thought that over. Then a small voice piped up and said, "How much would you offer me not to love my big sister?"

Humor aside, that minister was right on target. Unconditional love isn't free, but the price isn't paid in dollars and cents.

Our Greatest Fear

What do you suppose is the greatest fear of most people? I'm convinced that if we were to carry signs expressing it, they would read, "Please don't reject me." Experts say that the cars we drive, the homes we live in, the clothes we wear, and the games we play are all a part of trying to gain acceptance.

As Albert Schweitzer said, "The tragedy of life is not that we die, but rather what dies inside a man while he lives." When we feel rejected and unloved, something dies inside us.

The greatest terror children can have is that they're not loved; rejection is their idea of hell. And when they feel rejected, they get angry. Angry kids tend to get into trouble. Kids in trouble feel guilty. And with guilt comes rejection, which starts the cycle all over again.

Rejection doesn't affect just the rejected person, either. It's like an unbearable weight that we have to pass on to others. You can check it out—those who have been rejected tend to reject others. Rejection has a domino effect, and somewhere we have to break the cycle. We can be the ones to start that process for people close to us.

This will only happen, though, if we take time to love. Often, despite having the best intentions, we forget to do it. A scene in Thornton Wilder's play "Our Town" really brings that point home.

> *The tragedy of life is not that we die, but rather what dies inside a man while he lives.*

In the play, a girl named Emily dies, and then she's given a chance to return to earth and relive one day. She's asked which day she wants it to be, and she says, "Oh, I'd like for it to be my 12th birthday."

All the other dead people in the graveyard beg her, "Emily, don't do it! Emily, no!"

She answers, "But I want to see my mama and papa again."

So she returns to that day and comes down the stairs in her pretty dress. But her mother is busy making the birthday cake, so she doesn't notice. Emily says, "Mom, look at me. I'm the birthday girl."

"Fine, birthday girl," her mother answers, "sit down and eat your breakfast."

Emily stands there and says, "Mom, look at me!"

But Mom doesn't look. Then Dad comes through the house, but he doesn't look, either, because he's busy making money for her. And her big brothers sure don't look.

The scene ends with Emily standing in the middle of the house and saying, "Please, please, will somebody look at me? I don't need your cake and I don't need your money. Please just look at me." Nobody does, so she turns to her mother one more time and says, "Please, Mom."

Finally, Emily turns to the stage hand and says, "Take me

away. I forgot what it was like to be a human. Nobody looks at nobody. Nobody cares anymore, do they?"

The answer to her question is yes, we care. But we often forget to show it because we often forget what's really important. It's easy to get off on tangents, things that may even be good by themselves but that aren't the best use of our time and energy. We can get so wrapped up in doing things for others that we forget to do the simple but so-important things *with* them: looking them in the eye and listening with our full attention; putting an arm around their shoulder; saying "thank you" and "I couldn't make it without you."

The Bible says that loving God first and then loving our neihbors—those close to us—fulfills all the law. I wrote earlier about the need to set good goals and then pursue them with hope and persistence. Some of our goals should be in this area of how best to show our love every day to our family, friends and co-workers.

How to Say "I Love You"

That elderly couple who had honeymooned in room 803 found a wonderful way to express their love for each other. Another way I heard about came from the late Coach Scruggs, one of the great men of Abilene.

Coach Scruggs and his lae wife were in the audience where I spoke night, and afterward she came up to me and said, "Listen, I have to tell you something. We used to live in the barracks over here when we were in school, and Coach was in charge of the lights. We were dating, and every night he had to turn the lights out at 10. He would always flick 'em three times, and it meant 'I love you.'

"All through our married life, he would just come by, and maybe I'd be sitting around, or baking or washing dishes and he would just tap me three times on my shoulder. We both understood the three words the taps represented."

Isn't that a beautiful way to express enduring love? There are a lot of ways to do it, as many as our minds can imagine.

But we've got to find the way or ways that work for us in our relationships. The giving of such unconditional love is at the very heart of what it means to be human and to be made in God's image.

Let me tell you one more story of a marvelous, miraculous way a man found to express his love. Geno Calabreezy was in the hospital with terminal cancer. His wife of 36 years was constantly by his bedside. She left only when it was absolutely necessary.

One Sunday afternoon, she was so exhausted that as she sat next to his bed, holding his hand, she put her head down and fell asleep. We don't know exactly what happened next, but obviously Geno came out of his coma. He must have reached over with his left hand (his wife was holding his right and he wasn't left-handed,) picked up an envelope, and written some words on it.

When his wife awoke, Geno was dead. But he was clutching that envelope, and the words on that envelope were so beautiful that someone set them to music.

You may have heard them—Frank Sinatra made a famous recording of the song. If you don't know the story behind the words, they might sound as if the writer were trying to tiptoe out of a condo at 2:30 in the morning with his shoes in his hand. But that's not what the story was about at all. It was about a loving, caring husband whose love never failed, not even as he lay dying.

The words on that envelope read, "Softly I leave you, for my heart would break if I should wake and see you go. So I leave you softly, long before you miss me—long before your arms can beg me stay for one more hour or one more day. And after all the years, I can't bear the tears to fall, so I leave you softly. So I leave you there."

That's the true story behind the song. May we all find our own ways to express unfailing love.

Chapter Reflection

The theme of this chapter is love never fails. Do you know of a love between two people that *never* fails? What would be some attributes of such a love?

Discussion Questions

1. In a time when divorce is at record levels, how can people develop a love that "never lets others down"? Why does love seem to fail so often?

2. How are God and Christ our examples of unfailing love? Can you recall any scriptures relating to this constancy?

3. Read Deuteronomy 7:9, 1 Corinthians 10:13, 2 Timothy 2:13 and John 10:11-15. Sum up these passages in your own words.

4. In Mark 12:28-31, Christ said the first commandment is to love God and the second commandment is to love our brothers. Why do you think that He focused on our loving God and others instead of focusing on any number of other things? What is so fundamental about love? What does the love principle say about God and His people?

5. How does a person develop a faithful and durable love?

13

You Can't Live Any Better Than You Can Love

Love life and life will love you back.
Love people and they will love you back.
(Arthur Rubenstein)

Bishop Gerald Kennedy told a story about a time years ago when he was on a speaking tour in Australia. He was working hard, spending every spare minute in preparation for the next engagement. One morning when the maid came to clean his room, he took a chair out in the hall and continued to work there.

As he was trying to concentrate, someone in an adjoining room began to play the violin. That really annoyed Kennedy because he had so much to do. He picked up his chair and went back into the room, complaining to himself.

The maid overheard him and said, "Oh, Mr. Kennedy, do you know who that is playing the violin?"

"No, I don't," he said. "Who is it?"

"Why, Mr. Kennedy," she answered, "it's Yehudi Menuhin, the world-famous violinist. He's getting ready for a concert tonight."

Kennedy was shocked. He couldn't believe it. But he took his chair back into the hall and just sat there, listening to the great artist rehearse. "It was a wonderful concert," he said, "the most beautiful music I'd heard in my entire life—once I realized who was playing."

There's music going on in the background of this life that we're usually not even aware of—invisible, out of sight. All the time it's playing wonderfully, just waiting for us to listen and enjoy, if we only know enough to tune in. And once we realize who the unseen Guest is that's playing, we'll never look at life the same again. This is the music of love.

Let's face it: the way most of us live is not really life. We're just going through the motions in what might be called a living death. And the really sad thing is that most of us don't know what to do about it. The answer is learning to love. As I said at the very beginning of this book, we can't live any better than we can love. We read at the end of 1 Corinthians 13, "And now these three remain: faith, hope and love. But the greatest of these is love" (v. 13).

> ". . . and the greatest of these is love."

Albert Einstein spent the last 30 years of his intellectually brilliant life in a gallant attempt to formulate a unifying theory that would explain all dimensions of physics, but he never succeeded. Likewise, I doubt that the human personality will ever be reduced to a single explanation. We're far too complex to be simplified that way.

From another perspective, however, there is one key to all human relationships. Of course, it is love. Conflicts seem to resolve themselves when people live according to 1 Corinthians 13, avoiding boastfulness, envying, vengefulness, impatience and rudeness. That one chapter offers the ultimate prescription for harmonious living. No new discovery will ever improve upon it.

The Healing, Hopeful Power of Love

A woman lost her husband and was having trouble moving through the stages of grief. For weeks, she went every day to the cemetery to put flowers on his grave. She simply could not let go. No matter what she did, it seemed grief would never leave her.

In despair, she went to her doctor for a checkup and told him about taking flowers to the cemetery every day. He responded with a gentle suggestion. "Instead of taking flowers to the cemetery," he said, "why don't you take them to the hospital? I have two patients there who are alone. They have no family in the city, and they would really enjoy receiving some fresh flowers. Why not take the flowers to them for one day, ask them about their progress, give them some encouragement, and see if there's anything you can do for them?"

The lady took her doctor's suggestion. The next day, she carried flowers to the hospital rather than to the cemetery. She continued to do that, and before long, she was able to work through her grief.

No matter the difficulty, if we have enough love, it will help us to overcome. There is no door that will not open if we'll give and receive love. There is no gulf large enough that love can't breach it. No problem or crisis or hopeless situation will keep us from being the happiest, most fulfilled creatures in the world if we learn to love.

Abraham Lincoln went by the slave block one day and saw a young girl being put up for sale. He decided to redeem her and so put in a bid. As the girl looked at the tall, homely, white man trying to buy her, she figured he was just another slave owner who intended to take her and abuse her.

Lincoln won the bidding and paid for the girl. As they walked away together, he told her, "Young lady, you're free."

"What does that mean?" she asked.

"It means you're free," he answered.

"Does that mean I can say whatever I want to say?"

"Yes, my dear, you can say anything you want to say."

"Does that mean I can be anything I want to be?"

"Yes, you can be anything you want to be."

"Does that mean I can go anywhere I want to go?"

"Yes, you can go anywhere you want to go."

With tears now streaming down her face, she told him, "Then I'll go with you."

Love is the greatest. It's simply the most powerful force in the universe. Even small, simple amounts of it can do wonders. Consider the story of Stan Cottrell. He's a long-distance runner, and I do mean long. He ran all over China, starting at the Great Wall, over the mountains, into the interior, and through villages where few outsiders have ever gone.

Stan ran 53 consecutive days, averaging 40 miles a day. That's like two marathons a day for 53 days in a row! (I ran a marathon once; I got over the urge.) He covered more than 1,000 miles in driving rain and hot sun, and with a cracked vertebra, bleeding feet, nerves on end and excruciating pain.

Not surprisingly, Stan faced numerous times when the pain got so bad that he knew he had to stop. But just when he was about to quit, someone would come running up and say, "There are many people waiting for you in the next village, and your coming will bring endless joy." Hearing that, Stan's spirits would soar, and he would push on to that next village.

There's power in that pull of love, knowing someone is rooting for you, waiting for you and counting on you.

Charlie Brown picked up the ringing phone one time in a "Peanuts" cartoon. A female voice on the other end said, "Charlie Brown, we're going to miss you. Marcy and I are going to camp, and we're going to be swimming instructors."

Then Marcy took the phone and said, "Charles, we just called to say good-bye and that we love you."

And that loser Charlie Brown stood there with a grin from ear to ear. Someone asked him, "Who was that?"

"I think it was a right number," he said. Love is always a right number. Always.

Never a Trifle

Michelangelo was one of the world's all-time great painters, probably best known for his work on the ceiling of the Sistine Chapel in the Vatican. But he was also a great sculptor. And one day, a visitor was looking at a statue he was creating in his studio.

You Can't Live Any Better Than You Can Love

The visitor said, "I can't see that you've made any progress since I was here the last time."

"Oh, yes, I've made much progress," Michelangelo answered. "Look carefully and you'll see that I have retouched this part and polished that. I have also worked on this part, and I've softened the lines here."

"Yes," said the visitor, "but these are all trifles."

"That may be," replied Michelangelo, "but trifles make perfection, and perfection is no trifle."

I hope that you now understand that love can be expressed in a thousand different, simple ways. Sometimes the little aspects like kindness, encouragement and optimism seem so small, but genuine love is never a trifle. And a lifetime of adding up and unifying all those efforts will turn out to be a beautiful piece of enduring art.

Isaac Watts, who wrote many of the beautiful hymns we sing in our worship services, lived next door to an elderly lady and visited her often. No wonder; she paid him so much attention. One day, while he was in her home, he kept admiring a plaque on her wall.

> *God loves you so much He can't keep His eyes off you.*

"Isaac," she said, "I want to give you that plaque. I've watched you look at it, and I want you to have it."

The plaque read, "Thou God seest me," from Genesis 16:13.

The lady went on, "Now, Isaac, people are going to tell you that verse means God is looking over your shoulder, trying to catch you doing something wrong. But don't you believe them. Isaac, what it means is that God loves you so much, He can't keep His eyes off you."

If that's a proper interpretation of the scripture, and I think it is, I'm just now beginning to understand it because I've just been experiencing the love of grandchildren for a few years. I respond to them much differently than I did with my own children.

I see them almost every day, and I can happily watch them for hours. Do I do that so I can catch them doing something wrong? Oh, no! I watch them because I love them so much I can't keep my eyes off them. And God loves me more than I love my grandchildren.

We used to sing, "There's an all-seeing eye watching you." We bred fear and guilt in everybody. But God isn't waiting to jump on us. He "jumped on" His Son so He wouldn't have to condemn us, and He did it while we were yet sinners, in open rebellion against Him. He admires and loves us so much that He can't take His eyes off us. How beautiful that thought is, and how much it frees us to love others in return. That's why we want to love and follow Him as directed in His Word, with all our hearts, for all our lives.

We really can't live any better than we can love. But with God's help—my, how we can love!

Chapter Reflection

Webster defines a habit as "an acquired behavior pattern regularly followed until it has become almost involuntary." Twelve habits of the heart have been discussed in the preceding chapters. Each of these habits, by definition, is acquired over time. Reflect on the habits listed below. Can you identify any of these habits that need your attention more than others?
1. Doing the right thing for the right reason.
2. Giving the gift of courtesy.
3. Rejoicing, not being resentful.
4. Showing true humility.
5. Encouraging others.
6. Keeping a long fuse.
7. Holding no grudges.
8. Drawn to the truth.
9. Always optimistic.
10. Willing to persevere.
11. Never letting others down.
12. You can't live any better than you can love.